Women and Autobiography
in the T

Women and Autobiography in the Twentieth Century

Remembered Futures

Linda Anderson

PRENTICE HALL

HARVESTER WHEATSHEAF

London New York Toronto Sydney Tokyo Singapore
Madrid Mexico City Munich

First published 1997 by
Prentice Hall/Harvester Wheatsheaf
Campus 400, Maylands Avenue
Hemel Hempstead
Hertfordshire, HP2 7EZ
A division of
Simon & Schuster International Group

Typeset in 10/12pt Times
by Hands Fotoset, Leicester

Printed and bound in Great Britain by
TJ Press (Padstow) Ltd, Padstow, Cornwall

Library of Congress Cataloging-in-Publication Data

Anderson, Linda, 1950–
   Women and autobiography in the twentieth century / Linda Anderson.
      p.   cm.
   Includes bibliographical references (p.   ) and index.
   ISBN 0-13-355034-6 (pbk.)
   1. Autobiography—Women authors.   2. English prose literature–
–Women authors—History and criticism.   3. American prose
literature—Women authors—History and criticism.   4. Women authors,
English—20th century—Biography—History and criticism.   5. Women
authors, American—20th century—Biography—History and criticism.
6. Women—Great Britain—Biography—History and criticism.
7. Women—United States—Biography—History and criticism.
8. James, Alice, 1848–1892—Biography.   9. Woolf, Virginia,
1882–1941—Biography.   10. Brittain, Vera, 1983–1970—Biography.
11. Plath, Sylvia—Biography.   12, Feminism—Historiography.
I. Title.
PR808.W65A53   1996
828′.910809492072—dc20   96–17070
                                                              CIP

British Library Cataloguing in Publication Data

A catalogue record for this book is available from
the British Library

ISBN 0-13-355034-6

---

1   2   3   4   5   01   00   99   98   97

Contents

For Vivienne

Acknowledgements

I am grateful to the Research Committee of the University of Newcastle upon Tyne for funding for this project. I also want to express my gratitude to students and staff at the Universities of Aberdeen, Lancaster, Nottingham, Sussex and York for invitations to speak on the topic of 'Women and Autobiography' and for the many helpful suggestions and comments I received on these occasions.

Many friends and colleagues have been a source of solace, support and inspiration during the writing of this book. I want to thank Margaret Beetham, Treva Broughton, Terry Castle, Penny Florence, Rima Handley, Judith Hawley, Desmond Graham, Nicole Ward Jouve, Gordon MacMullan, Gill Plain, Clare Tarplee, Lizzie Thynne, Margaret Wilkinson and Sylvia Wilson. Sue Roe believed in the idea of this book and enlivened my original thinking about it. Jackie Jones showed exemplary patience and understanding during its long gestation and I am grateful to her for her encouragement. Cynthia Fuller's friendship over the years has enriched both my life and my writing. To Ann Spencer I owe special thanks for her thoughtful and nurturing friendship during the final stages of this book. Finally, Vivienne Morris helped me to discover how much creative potential there is in 'remembering the future'. I am deeply grateful to her for her wisdom and support.

Extracts from Alice James's unpublished letters are reproduced with permission of Alexander R. James Jr., the Houghton Library,

Harvard University and The Trustees of the National Library of Scotland.

Acknowledgement is made to the Estate of Virginia Woolf and Chatto and Windus for permission to quote from Virginia Woolf's *Diary* and from *Moments of Being*.

CHAPTER ONE

Introduction

> You can go home again . . . so long as you understand that home is
> a place where you have never been.
>
> Ursula K. Le Guin, *The Dispossessed*

> Writing is not arriving; most of the time it's *not arriving*. One must
> go on foot, with the body . . . One must walk as far as the night.
> One's own night. Walking through the self toward the dark.
>
> Hélène Cixous, *Three Steps on the Ladder of Writing*

> It is at the door, looking in, that I always see myself, in memory.
>
> Louise Bogan, *Journey Around My Room*

Feminist criticism and women's autobiography

In her article, 'Autobiography in the Aftermath of Romanticism',
published in 1982, Candace Lang took issue with the 'man-behind-
the-work' approach of many critics of autobiography.[1] For Lang,
part of what this 'realist expressive' model of autobiography failed
to comprehend was how much the autobiographer and the critic
share with each other.[2] Language was the common thread, or rather
an increasingly precocious knowledge of how language shaped and
limited their projects. According to Lang, both the meta-language
of criticism and autobiographical discourse 'must ultimately pose
the same problems; for both criticism and autobiography are
discourses of language on – "about" – language'.[3]

Lang's article emerges in the wake of another 'ism' – poststructuralism – which could be said to have announced, along with
the 'death of the author', a transformation in how we view the
autobiographical subject. Lang's point is that what makes the
autobiographer a reader or critic of how 'he' signifies in social and
linguistic terms – the collapsing of the distinction between subject
and language – turns the critic, who is no longer able to sustain his
interpretive distance, into an autobiographer. Both begin to teeter
on the edge of tautology or the madness of a discourse which offers
neither of them a way out of its all-encompassing web.

But what of feminist criticism? Or the relation between women as writers and readers of autobiography? In the symbiotic merger Lang envisages between the autobiographer and the critic, there is no space left for the interposition of sexual difference. Prising apart this apparent seamlessness – recognising the absence of women writers from the autobiographical canon, or of gender from critical accounts of autobiography – has been the major enterprise of feminist study of autobiography for more than a decade. In 1980, introducing *Women's Autobiography*, the first collection of essays devoted exclusively to this topic, Estelle Jelinek wrote of the 'excellent and innovative autobiographies by women that have been ignored or excluded from the critical canon' as well as noting the dearth of critical material on women's autobiography up till then.[4] In 1984, Domna Stanton – moving away from Jelinek's gynocritical model, though sharing her political motivation – exposed how autobiography as a genre, or as a set of definitions and traditions aimed at stabilising and legitimating texts, privileged the masculine subject, at the same time as she suggested how woman's very illegitimacy – her fraudulent presence within the symbolic order – could become the mark of her autobiographical difference.[5]

Since then things have moved on, though many of the same issues tend to recur. The rapid proliferation of studies on women's autobiography in recent years has proved how extensive, both historically and geographically, women's autobiographical writing is.[6] Through the late 1980s and early 1990s critics have also explored, with increasing sophistication and in the context of recent critical theory, how women can represent themselves in terms of a genre which *as* genre – rather than as something 'homelier' or less literary, like diaries or letters[7] – derives its coherence from the unity of the self, from a self which transcends inconsistency and difference.[8] As this suggests, the identity of autobiography as a genre – less a matter of form and aesthetics than of ideology – is put into question in a feminist critique of autobiography as well as (or because of) how 'she' identifies as 'I', that is takes up a position in writing which she cannot 'naturally' assume. Yet, if one of the main areas of focus has been 'the difficulty of saying "I"'[9] for women autobiographers, it is impossible to separate this in the end from the difficulty of saying 'she'; in other words the construction of women as autobiographical subjects is inevitably implicated in –

or a part of – the fluctuating discourses which construct the meaning of gender itself.

This book, as a study of women's autobiographical writing in the twentieth century, situates itself at this same moment of critical debate when the very terms in which women's autobiographical writing can be thought must also be held open to critical interrogation. But like other writers on this topic I feel the need to hesitate here, not quite sure that the radical potential of women's autobiographical writing can be defined in this theoretical way; that, however destabilised the critical terms, they do not effect some form of closure around the texts themselves. This point could be seen as a political one: as Bella Brodski and Celeste Schenk have declared, posing the limits of a deconstructive critical practice: 'A feminist agenda cannot include further or repeated marginalization of female selfhood without betraying its own political program.'[10] The same point has been made by Nancy Miller when she questions whether the 'postmodern decision that the Author is dead' should apply equally to women: 'Because women have not had the same historical relation of identity to origin, institution, production that men have had, they have not, I think (collectively) felt burdened by too much Self, Ego, Cogito, etc.'[11] For these critics, a deconstructive approach to the subject may deprive us of ways of thinking about how women's writing, but autobiography in particular, enacts an active appropriation of identity – the laying claim to both a life and a text – even as it provides the means of opening up both the self and writing to questions of difference.

At this point, however, let us go back to the relationship between feminist criticism and women's autobiography in more general terms. In her *Speculum of the Other Woman* Luce Irigaray has provocatively claimed that 'any theory of the subject has always been appropriated by the "masculine"'. For Irigaray, such theoretical discourses, whilst they present themselves as neutral or objective, also cover or veil a partiality which is revealed in their (unconscious) positioning of women as material or object. When a woman, therefore, 'submits to (such a) theory' she 'fails to realize that she is renouncing the specificity of her own relationship to the imaginary'.[12] Irigaray's project is also to attempt to posit a new feminine subject, to find representational systems in which women's identities can be constructed in different ways; like the critics of autobiography we have mentioned, therefore, she wants to affirm, beyond deconstruction, the possibility of a new subjectivity for women, a subjectivity which is not simply the repressed of male discourse, but which *could be expressed*. At the same time, however, she seems to suggest an insoluble problem about women's relation to theory, a problem which could be summed up in the questions: where does the woman speak from? who does she speak for? In other words, how can a woman take up a stance within theory – attempt to theorise women – without repeating the very gesture which has traditionally deprived women of a voice, of their 'own relationship to the imaginary'? How can she speak for women without also assigning them the status of object within her own discourse? In thinking about the relation between criticism and autobiography, then, it could be we are beginning to define a contradiction, or a paradox: for a feminist criticism of autobiography could well be attempting to speak for – about – those very discourses where women might best be seen as speaking for themselves.

Let me now change the focus. Another moment of hesitation. This time a critical essay, not about autobiography, but about women's relation to poetry. In 'When We Dead Awaken: Writing as Re-Vision', first delivered as a lecture in 1971, Adrienne Rich pauses for a moment of self-reflection as her writing (or speech) begins to take an autobiographical turn. 'I have hesitated to do what I am going to do now which is to use myself as illustration. For one thing it's a lot easier and less dangerous to talk about other women writers.'[13] Since then other feminist critics have taken the same introspective route, choosing, despite the dangers, to 'use themselves as illustration'. A book entitled *Between Women*, published in 1984, consists entirely of that, of a number of American women scholars 'getting personal'[14] about their work. Critical and personal engagement are interwoven in the stories collected here: 'Virginia Woolf changed my life', Sarah Ruddick confesses simply at the beginning of her essay.[15] For the editors the project seems twofold: the personal narratives, by the very form they take, implicitly question the division between knowledge and life, objectivity and intimacy. But the essays at the same time return to the issue of how to negotiate the distance between subject and object, critic and woman artist, as an explicit concern, attempting in the process to rethink the role of subjectivity in scholarship: 'If we submit to identification self-consciously and reflect on the process rather than fighting it, what do we learn?'[16]

The inclusion of personal reflections and more extended autobiographical narratives within feminist criticism has become a commonplace yet we could see it as a historical phenomenon as well, predating a critical interest in women's autobiography as a literary genre or form. From this point of view it seems to belong – though not exclusively – to a particular moment within feminist criticism, an era before the break which Mary Jacobus marks in the mid 1970s when French theory 'infiltrated and often polarized feminist literary criticism'.[17] Writing autobiographically could be seen as the attempt, in the early stages of feminism, of writing explicitly *as a woman*, of – like consciousness-raising – grounding perception in the experiences and problems which seemed to provide women with a sense of identity as a group.[18] Looking back, from within a later and more self-conscious version of 'personal criticism' in the 1990s, Nancy Miller has argued that feminist theory has 'always built out from the personal' and that '"the authority of experience"' which founded 'a central current in feminist theory in the 1970s' still 'continues – dismantled and renovated – to shape a variety of personal and less personal discourses at an oppositional angle to dominant critical positionings'.[19] Yet Miller, for all her recognition of the excitement that went – perhaps still goes – with the finding of a community by women, or by any oppressed group, is wary of the 'speaking as a' claim which, while it challenges the notion of a subject position which is universal, can also elide differences beneath a false representativity. Her own version of 'personal criticism' she sees as a form of 'autobiographical performance in the act of criticism'.[20] The inclusion of the word *performance* is important since it suggests the taking up of a position – an 'as if' rather than an 'as a' – a deliberate exposure of the critic as figure within the text not, as Miller argues, in order to displace theory but to speak personally within it and about it, uncovering its impersonality as a mask for another fiction of the self. Miller uses the word 'engaged' to move her 'performance' beyond the realm of the signifier, attempting to invoke an ethics of speaking out, of disturbance and risk. Yet, whilst her own personal style of criticism overcomes some of the problems involved in claiming authenticity for writing by reference to a pre-discursive identity and also challenges the impersonal critic to show his/her face, there is a problem that, in institutionalised form, the risk of 'personal criticism' could extend no further than the substitution of one style of academic authority for another.[21]

Shoshana Felman is right, I think, to ask us to return to those earlier moments within feminist criticism, when autobiography first broke into critical texts, creating a hiatus, or a hesitation between two forms of discourse. The point Felman makes about Adrienne Rich's essay, 'When We Dead Awaken', that we looked at earlier, is that, before autobiography is used by Rich to authorise her writing, she resists it, 'inscribing her hesistation', as Felman puts it, 'permanently into the text'. Whilst autobiography resists theory, at this threshold between them theory equally resists autobiography: 'What is at stake is not merely the combination of autobiography and theory but their interaction: not merely their mutual informa-tion but their mutual transformation.'[22] The same point could be made about the other example I referred to: the editors of *Between Women* encourage not only identification as a critical model but self-conscious reflection on the process; they offer a model not of resistance to subjectivity – 'fighting it' – but a resistance within subjectivity, a tension or a distance between two modes of self-consciousness.

Felman wants to alert us to the problematics of autobiography, to the ways in which a woman's autobiography can only be thought about as a narrative which has not yet come into being: 'Trained to see ourselves as objects and to be positioned as the Other, estranged to ourselves, we have a story that by definition cannot be self-present to us, a story that, in other words, is not a story, but must become a story.'[23] Moments of dissonance between different discourses, the moments when autobiography resists theory, personalising its utterance, or when theory interrupts auto-biography with the knowledge of what it cannot say, are also moments when the 'not yet' of the female subject is written into the text. But what might this mean for a feminist criticism *of* autobiography? For the relationship between writing and reading subjects?

A model – such as the one Felman uses – of returning to texts in order to discover meanings which were previously overlooked or forgotten makes the critic into a witness less to what a text says than what it *will* say in the future. If there is a gap within autobiography – as Felman proposes – between what gets written and the knowledge of it that is assimilable at the time, if autobiography also communicates its knowledge of the female subject as, in part, the impossibility of *having* that knowledge, criticism becomes the act of attempting to read into the future what was 'not yet' in the past. This is the nature of the relation or space evoked by Christa Wolf in her novel, *The Quest for Christa T*, where the narrator not only elegises her friend, but searches for her through vague and fragmented memories which can only begin to release their meaning later; what she beckons into her own writing is the potential or sense of becoming, the not fully realised self who has inscribed her future in the past:[24]

> Now out she came, calm even in the unfulfillment of her wishes, for she had the strength to say: Not yet. She carried many lives around her, storing them in herself; and in herself she stored many times as well, times in which she lived partially unknown, as was the case in her 'real' time; and what is not possible in one time becomes real in another. But she called all her various times serenely: Our time.[25]

Christa T. cannot be objectified by the narrator or the past reified since memory turns out not to be static; in the narrator's memories of her, Christa T. is still creating herself. Moreover, in her struggle to understand the narrator must acknowledge how her memories of her friend exceed the available models of understanding; that her memories contain knowledge that she has not yet gained access to. 'Our time' – so simply stated but, as a phrase, holding within itself complex depths – could mean not only the way historical time is interfused by a subjective yearning to exist beyond its frame but, in the context of the book, the time created by intersubjectivity, the movement between different stances towards time and different kinds of knowledge.[26]

Wolf's narrative undoes the hierarchical relation of subject and object, preserving Christa T.'s autonomy in relation to her interpreter by suggesting the ways her self-creation – her imaginative openness to the possibilities of her life – make the narrator think, or remember, again. This is linked, of course, to the problems I am attempting to address in this introduction; it takes us back, I believe, to Irigaray's contention about the impossibility of women having, or creating, their different relation to their imaginary – and thus of becoming subjects – within discourses which only leave room for one 'logical' way of ordering the relation between subject and object. The idea that the reader may be hearing in an autobiographical text something that cannot be present to the self – a memory yet to be understood, a potential yet to come into being – could suggest ways in which the reader's knowledge too must be constructed through gaps and unconscious desires – in other words be formulated in terms of the shape and horizons of memory. Might it be possible to think about memory as creating a space, in Irigaray's terms, for 'woman's relation to the imaginary'? As suspending itself between writer and reader, awaiting decipherment? The idea that I am tentatively putting forward is not to do with the reader merging her own memories with those of the text, reading her own 'self' there – nor even critically performing her own personal stance within her writing – but with how a feminist reading of autobiography could 'include' memory, or create a space *like* memory, where past and future meet.

The space of memory

The structural significance of memory for writers and readers of women's autobiography might seem, however, to beg another question: what is it that women are trying to remember? What is it that they might have forgotten?

By way of an answer I want to turn to one of the autobiographers I will be considering in this book. Alice James noted in her diary in 1889 that, since she had only 'little bits' of insignificant memory rather than 'great ones', 'it all seems like a reminiscence'. She then went on to evoke the sense of memory filling her consciousness: 'As I go along the childish impressions of light and colour come crowding back into my mind and with them the expectant, which then palpitated within me, lives for a ghostly moment'.[27] According to Freud's and Breuer's famous definition of hysteria – 'hysterics suffer mainly from reminiscence' – Alice James's preoccupation with memory could be seen as a pathological or hysterical symptom, a sign of the neurotic attachment to the past which accompanies a disavowal of heterosexual desire.[28] Unable to take up her 'normal' adult position within the symbolic, the hysteric for Freud, was also unable to put the past behind her, but was condemned to live it, endlessly, repetitively, retreating from historical or linear time into a phantasmal past.

Elizabeth Grosz draws a distinction between the hysteric's repression of heterosexual desire – Freud's view – and what could be seen as her refusal of it.[29] From a feminist perspective the hysteric is sick with (of) her pathological position within the symbolic order which both defines her through lack or passivity and cuts her off from her pre-oedipal attachment to her mother. Her sickness is a symptom of a sickness which might thus be more accurately attributed to the symbolic itself. The woman's turning towards the past could also be taken, therefore, as a gesture of regret towards the present and towards a symbolic system, which, constructed only in terms of the masculine subject, denies her a place or a home within it.[30]

When does remembering turn into nostalgic longing? And is nostalgia a particularly female form of remembrance? Mary Jacobus, in an essay where she explores women's relation to the pre-oedipal, takes Freud's linking of homesickness to an unconscious memory of the mother's body and attempts to interpret its 'specifically feminine dimension'.[31] Nostalgia, for Jacobus, is defined as 'a longing for what one never had'. Later in the essay, she adds to this by reference to Jane Gallop's formulation of the meaning of *nostalgie* in French: 'Haunting regret for one's native land or homesickness'.[32] For Jacobus, both feminine nostalgia for, and feminist theorising about the mother, are set in motion by an 'imaginary deprivation' or a myth since the pre-oedipal relation to the mother can only be recalled from the other side of the Oedipal crisis; in other words, the notion of a lost plenitude can only be constructed after the event and projected back into a past which, for the subject, never existed. The mother never was phallic, but structured, even in the pre-oedipal phase, through division and lack. Both the girl's relation to castration and to the idea of the mother's wholeness, perceived in terms of loss, are in effect, therefore, a nostalgic desire for what never was. If, as within this Lacanian model, the subject is always structured through division and lack, then nostalgia comes to denote simply 'the feminine articulation of what it means to be a gendered subject'.[33]

Jacobus also uses these ideas to read Virginia Woolf's *To The Lighthouse*, and in particular Lily Briscoe's nostalgic longing for Mrs Ramsay or the absent mother. The scene at the end of the novel, as Lily paints her painting, feeling, at the same time the agony of her own unassuageable desire, enacts, according to

Jacobus, the process by which the subject comes into being, identifying with the signs which cover the maternal void. The mother's absence is therefore a prerequisite of self-inscription: 'The price Lily pays for finishing her picture is the casting out of the mother, her beloved Mrs Ramsay.'[34]

Yet there could be another way of looking at this picture. Without necessarily disagreeing with Jacobus' argument about the impossibility of a return to a state of psychic wholeness, it might still be posssible to rescue memory from nostalgia and to think about home as a destination – something yet to be constructed – and not as an origin we can only ever desire in retrospect. In other words, is there a way that women could discover a space within the symbolic for their subjectivity? Remember rather than be consigned to forgetfulness, to an unrepresentable outside?

In an essay entitled 'Flesh Colours', Luce Irigaray describes memory as 'the place where identity is formed, the place where each person builds his or her ground or territory'. She also in this same essay employs an analogy between the work of an analytic session and painting. According to Irigaray the analyst, listening to a patient should 'direct his or her attention not only to the repetition of former images and their possible interpretation, but also to build bridges, establish perspectives between present-past-future'.[35] This conversion of time into space – the attempt to make time simultaneous – provides a ground for the subject where imagination can flourish. Irigaray stresses the link between bodily perception – sound, colours and rhythms – and the capacity imaginatively to synthesise and produce new structures. It is for this reason that she seems to want to move analysis away from conceptualising itself solely in term of language: language tends towards abstraction; painting preserves more sensitively the qualities of the flesh and therefore of gender. The aim for Irigaray is an imaginative fluidity – a symbolic relation to the imaginary – which in the end could also change the meaning of sexual difference:

> We need to remember that sexual difference is not to be recognized only from signs or signifiers that have already been coded, which are, in any case, far from unchanging. Sexual difference also corresponds to the possibility of different perceptions and creations.[36]

Following Irigaray, therefore, it could be argued that an interpretation of Lily's painting in *To the Lighthouse* which sees it as occupying the same place as writing in the novel misses an important difference: painting creates a space which can hold both past and present simultaneously. As a new structuring of perspectives – of the relation between past, present and future – Lily's composition not only paints over the void of maternal absence; it could also be said to find a different way of painting Mrs Ramsay into the picture. The figure of the painting is, I would suggest, more than a figure for language; by painting the relation between herself and the maternal, Lily as artist – and Woolf through the imaging of her art – could also be seen as attempting to find a way of bringing colour – for Irigaray associated with the body – back into words.

A similar point could be made about the quotation from Alice James's diary that we looked at before: she too evokes a picture, spatialising memory, and endowing it with the immediate, vital qualities of light and colour. Memory is thus less a space which prevents an entry into time – in the way Freud and Breuer interpret it – than the ground which allows the imagining of a different time. Alice James is haunted less by the ghost of the past than her ghostly imagination of a future.

To go back for a moment to Irigaray's invocation of painting as an analogy for analysis: for Irigaray part of the point of this comparision is the question it raises about the role of interpretation. Irigaray is critical of the stress laid by classical psychoanalysis on the analytic function: 'If Freud considered the psychoanalytic cure to be interminable, it is because he thinks and interprets in terms of *analysis*, not discovery or creation.' The danger, for Irigaray, is that analysis *per se* interrupts, or even cuts into and destroys, the patient's subjectivity. Irigaray presents an alternative view of psychoanalytic interpretation: 'Interpretation can be defined as the ability to compose along with the patient and to help the patient to paint.'[37]

The idea that interpretation can happen *alongside* the recognition of the other's capacity for creativity, for the production of new formations, challenges both the role of interpretation and the structural authority of the analyst as someone who has the power to interpret. That this has an implication for women is clear, as we have already seen from Irigaray's more general understanding of the gendering of theoretical discourse as well as her – and other feminists' – critique of psychoanalysis for its phallocentric bias. What interests me here in particular, however, is more the way

Irigaray uses *memory* to suspend the power of interpretation, creating a space between analyst and patient for the patient's potential to emerge. This, I think, is not, or not necessarily, to deny memory's troubled relation to the past, of how it represents, in the way Mary Jacobus has described, a past which it also veils or denies. However, the recognition that memory could also provide a space in which the subject can create herself, or that it contains a future we have yet to gain access to, could also change the knowledge we already have. It may be that a woman is not necessarily condemned to repeat the past that psychoanalytic and other discourses have interpreted for her and constructed her through.

Remembered futures

In the chapters that follow I have not attempted to write a history of women's autobiographical writing in the twentieth century, nor have I tried to develop an overarching theory about it. Instead I have let problems of theory and interpretation present themselves to me in the course of reading and writing about the texts. At times it has felt necessary to engage with particular ideas in order to uncover what they can and cannot say about the relation between subjectivity, gender and writing, even if it took me away from the particularities of the text I was discussing. At other moments it has been important not to hold that interpretive position but to read alongside the texts in a more descriptive way in an attempt to allow their 'future' meanings to emerge. I have also not felt constrained by definitions of autobiography as a genre, which in any case tend to perpetuate a masculine genealogy of the subject, but have included here different kinds of autobiographical writing – diaries, letters, fiction and theoretical writing – under the general umbrella of autobiography. Part of the point of the book, of course, is precisely to understand the ways in which women's writing may position itself at different or oblique angles to dominant forms, interrogating the division between private and public writing, private and public 'selves'.

The issue of privacy is taken up in the next chapter. Alice James never published her diary in her lifetime though she may have had, as she was writing it, half an eye on her posthumous reputation. Thinking about her as a 'hysterical autobiographer', as I do in this chapter, returns us to questions of interpretation, to the discourses which form our understanding of gender and the subject. Alice James's physical frailty draws attention to questions of social and psychological restriction; at the same time, by miming certain plots within her life and writing, by deliberately adopting the roles she is given, she also exceeds them, gesturing towards other spaces which she could not fully represent.

In Chapter 3 I concentrate on Virginia Woolf's diary and the unpublished sketches in 'Moments of Being'. However it is important to recognise that throughout her work, in both fiction and non-fiction, Woolf was profoundly concerned with the problems of how to write a life, particularly a woman's life. Her unpublished autobiographical writings have an important connection with her experimentation elsewhere, opening spaces where she could eschew linearity and attempt to inscribe flux and process. Woolf's radicalism and importance as an autobiographer is precisely the extent to which she understood the connection between identity and writing and the need to deconstruct realist forms in order to create a space for the yet to be written feminine subject.

Chapter 4 explores the intersection betweeen the construction of gender relations during the First World War and the autobiographical possibilities it opened for women. In a sense Vera Brittain is able to take on a public role as autobiographer, in the way James and Woolf cannot, because she is also a witness for her generation, effacing her own claim to fame behind the memorial she creates for the young men who died. This raises questions about the relation between history and subjectivity, even as it reinscribes familar anxieties about public and private selves, and the writing of autobiography as both desire for, and transgression of, female subjecthood.

In Chapter 5 I look at the connection between fiction and autobiography. In a sense it is the publicity which has surrounded Sylvia Plath's life and death which has turned her novel, *The Bell Jar*, into an autobiography. There is a more general question here, of course, about how far autobiography is a question of *how* we read and whether we can ever read autobiography as other than fiction. The problem which Plath pursues within her writing, however, turns out to be precisely the invasiveness of the public realm; of how to create an identity in the face of culture's appropriation of the subject; or of how to write her femininity without simply rewriting society's violent inscription of the female body.

In the last chapter I return to some of the issues raised in this Introduction. Looking back to Adrienne Rich's *Of Woman Born* and Audre Lorde's *Zami* may make us question the utopian assumptions underlying the feminism of both texts, particularly their nostalgia towards the mother and the idea of home as well as the elision of their 'I' with a feminist 'we'. However, I believe difference is inscribed in both these texts through the questions they include about their own forms and meanings. I explore the difference between them as well as the differences within them and ask finally what place utopia should occupy within feminist autobiography.

Postscript

It is impossible to finish this Introduction without adding an autobiographical note of my own. This book has taken me a long time to complete because of events and changes within my own life. At times it has felt as if it has moved through many lives with me. Recently, however, I found myself saying to a friend: 'I think I've always been preoccupied with memory in my writing.' It was one of those moments when everything seemed to fall into a pattern. This, however, may be simply to repeat the themes of this Introduction: we write towards a future which we do not know but which may eventually know us differently.

CHAPTER TWO

Alice James: 'The subject is all that counts'[1]

Alice James, the only daughter in a family which boasted two famous sons, William and Henry, provides a dramatic example of the difficulties encountered by the woman who attempts to 'write herself'.[2] She began to keep her diary at the end of May 1889, at the age of 40; she kept it until her death in March 1892, recording her last entry two days before she died. Apart from letters and the commonplace book that preceded the diary this was to be her only literary work. The private status of the diary – though it seems to have been Alice's wish that it be published after her death[3] – leaves it unclear whether by naming herself in writing she was also seeking a name for herself as a writer. That this ambiguity existed for Alice too, offering her protection from what was, both culturally and psychologically, a daring act of self-assertion, is apparent from the very first entry that she wrote:

> My circumstances allowing of nothing but the ejaculation of one-syllabled reflections, a written monologue by that most interesting being, *myself*, may have its as yet to be discovered consolations. I shall at least have it all my own way and it may bring relief as an outlet to that geyser of emotions, sensations, speculations and reflections which ferments perpetually within my poor old carcass for its sins; so here goes, my first Journal! (p. 25)

The emphasis on 'myself' in this passage both draws attention to, and displaces attention from, the 'self' of the writer; the overemphasis also ironically undercuts the significance she is claiming for herself as 'that most interesting being'; writing becomes performance on a stage where she is also the audience, 'a monologue', what Nancy Miller has suggestively called in another context 'a posture of imposture'.[4] The power to define herself freely, 'to have it all my own way', is at odds with her own sense of power as a dangerously erupting (disrupting?) energy; power is not only what she can gain through writing but also what must be expelled in order to protect her weak (feminine) body. Throughout this very interesting passage Alice James uses language, tense with contradiction, which expresses both apology and potentiality: writing not only inscribes identity it also offers to her the possibility of redefinition. The problem she is eloquently and yet unconsciously expressing is how she as a woman can inhabit what she is also laying stake to through the act of writing itself, her own powerful imaginings and desires.

In 1889 when she began the diary Alice James was living in Leamington Spa, a fashionable resort for invalids who wished to 'take the waters'. Since coming to England from America in 1884 after her parents' death, Alice's health, always precarious, declined and she entered on a 'career' of invalidism, afflicted by pains which baffled her doctors and which they diagnosed variously as suppressed gout, neurasthenia, spinal neurosis and nervous hyperesthesia.[5] By 1886, as she wrote to her brother William, she foresaw little prospect of being able to return home: 'I see no chance of being well enough for the journey for a long time to come.'[6] By 1890 supposition had become reasonable certainty; in her diary, in a passage eulogising her brother Henry, she recalled that it was 'five years ago' that 'I suspended myself like an old woman of the sea round his neck where to all appearances I shall remain for all time.'[7] Increasingly it was death she looked to not just as an end, a closing off, but as the culmination of her life, a cure to uncertainty, the 'black future', giving shape and meaning to her life through its finality. Writing to William and his wife Alice in 1888 about the death of a mutual friend she expressed a sense of satisfaction: 'What an interest death lends to the most commonplace, making them so complete & clear-cut, all the vague & wobbly lines lost in the revelation of what they were meant to stand for'.[8] She greeted her aunt Kate's death with a similar observation, remarking on 'the new distinctness wh. the completion always gives'.[9] 'Death', she wrote could make the 'emptiness seem palpable'[10] and it was the 'palpable' nature of her own disease, cancer, diagnosed in 1891, bringing with it the imminent prospect of her death, which seemed to vindicate all that had preceded it, to offer resolution, even a curious sense of achievement. On 31 May 1891, she recorded in her diary that her 'aspirations' had been 'fulfilled':

> To him who waits, all things come! My aspirations may have been eccentric, but I cannot complain now, that they have not been brilliantly fulfilled. Ever since I have been ill, I have longed and longed for some palpable disease, no matter how conventionally dreadful a label it might have, but I was always driven back to stagger alone under the monstrous mass of subjective sensations. (p. 206)

The next day she commented on how the doctor, by his 'verdict' of cancer, had brought her 'enormous relief', 'lifting us out of the formless vague and setting us within the heart of the sustaining concrete' (p. 207). Perversely it is death and the promised nearness of her own extinction which brings solidity to her life. What these reactions to her doctor's diagnosis reveal is that the alternative to being defined as ill for Alice was to recoil in horror from her own subjectivity, to experience it without any vantage point, as formless or monstrous.[11]

In responding to death as also initiating meaning Alice James was discovering within her own life what some critics have considered to be the necessary conditions of narrative. Peter Brooks, for instance, has suggested that the meaning of narrative – the meaning that we as readers passionately seek – is only made possible through the fact of its ending:

> The very possibility of meaning plotted through time depends on the anticipated structuring force of the ending: the interminable would be meaningless . . . All narration is obituary in that life acquires definable meaning only at, and through, death.[12]

For Alice's brother Henry the problem of ending was the main problem he remembered having to overcome in writing his first novel, *Roderick Hudson*. Having perceived endlessly ramifying possibilities, he had to discover a 'geometry of his own' in which to enclose them; he had to structure his narrative towards an ending:

> For the prime effect of so sustained a system, so prepared a surface, is to lead on and on; while the fascination of following resides, by

the same token, in the presumability *somewhere* of a convenient, of a visibly-appointed stopping-place. Art would be easy indeed if, by a fond power disposed to 'patronise' it, such conveniences, such simplifications, had been provided. We have, as the case stands, to invent and establish them, to arrive at them by a difficult, dire process of selection and comparison, of surrender and sacrifice. The very meaning of expertness is acquired courage to brace one's self for the cruel crisis from the moment one sees it grimly loom.[13]

Henry James here, 'bracing himself for the cruel crisis', could well be writing about death and there is a way in which narrative closure needs to be referred to and understood as a premonition of our own death.[14] At the same time a distinction also holds: the death that Henry is writing about is figurative, Alice's is literal. Henry, writing his autobiography, came to see his life history in terms of the development of his artistic consciousness, recording his realisation that 'I should surely be good for nothing if not for projecting into the concrete' in language which uncannily echoes Alice's own discovery of the concretising value of death.[15] In a sense Alice could become an artist – could position herself as the triumphant Jamesian 'usurping consciousness'[16] – only if she were also the text, an object fashioned at last into meaning through no act of her own.[17] What Henry accomplished by his absorption in the process of art – 'it is art that *makes* life' he proclaimed at the end of his life[18] – Alice achieved through a complex act of splitting whereby she could be both body or mind to herself, subject or object, artist or text.

Catherine Belsey has proposed a clear relationship between this experience of internal splitting and society's ambivalent attitudes; writing in general terms, she sees women as a group necessarily caught between 'contradictory discourses':

> They participate both in the liberal humanist discourse of freedom, self-determination and rationality and at the same time in the specifically feminine discourse offered by society of submission, relative inadequacy and irrational intuition.[19]

This conflict, according to Alice James's biographer, Jean Strouse, was exaggerated within the James family: 'To be a James and a girl . . . was a contradiction in terms.'[20] Certainly Alice's writing, in her letters and her diary, reveals her constantly moving between different discourses. With her brothers, William and Henry, she shared a commitment to viewing her own perceptions and experience as both singular and significant. She was not wholly tongue-in-cheek when in 1891 in her diary she situated her 'achievement' alongside theirs:

> Within the last year he [Henry] has published *The Tragic Muse*, brought out *The American*, and written a play, *Mrs Vibert* (which Have has accepted) and his admirable comedy; combined with William's *Psychology*, not a bad show for one family! especially if I get myself dead, the hardest job of all. (p. 211)

If death becomes an end or an aim, then dying can also be seen in terms of 'success'; and if success can be measured in terms of the degree of personal difficulty endured, Alice's success could be said even to exceed her brothers'.

The encouragement to interpret success in such highly individual-istic terms came from Alice's father, Henry James Sr. He taught his children to apply a puritanical zeal to the cultivation of their 'selves'; ordinary living became an extraordinary effort to experi-ence and communicate intensely. His novelist son, who converted his father's precepts for living into an aesthetic creed, recalled in his autobiography that so far as his father was concerned the word 'spiritual' was 'the most living thing in the world for him – to the point that the spiritual simply meant to him the practical and the successful'. As a result particular choices of career could be seen as 'narrowing', as shutting the door on other 'spiritual' possibilities:

> What we were to do instead was just to *be* something, something unconnected with specific doing, something free and uncommitted, something finer in short than being *that*, whatever it was, might consist of.[21]

By this thinking failure and misfortune also constituted a form of 'success', creating perhaps even greater opportunities for the life of the spirit. For his father, there was 'scant measure of difference . . . for the life of the soul between the marked achievement and the marked shortcoming', Henry James observed.[22]

Henry James Sr's ideas, which had a serious impact on all his children, undoubtedly contributed to how Alice interpreted and justified her illness. When her brother William, having been told about her closeness to death, cast her in the role of victim and reflected on the difficulties and frustrations of her life, Alice felt the need to refute his point of view: what might be interpreted as failure from the outside, she affirmed, had been 'converted' inwardly into success:[23]

> You must . . . remember that a woman, by nature, needs much less to feed upon than a man, a few emotions & she is satisfied: so when I am gone, pray don't think of me simply as a creature who might have been something else had neurotic science been born; notwithstanding the poverty of my outside experience I have always had a significance for myself, & every chance to stumble along my straight & narrow little path, & to worship at the feet of my Deity, & what more can a human soul ask for?[24]

Conceding her difference as woman becomes a way, paradoxically, of asserting her superiority: because she needs less, Alice argues, the external becomes to a greater degree irrelevant to her; she can thus claim greater value for herself since value only exists internally, can only be established through its application to the self. She also demolishes William's position of 'knowledge' through science; whatever he knows he does not know her. In a sense Alice was turning his own ideas against him. It was William after all who was to write: 'Psychologically considered, our experiences resist conceptual reduction . . . Biography is the concrete form in which all that is is immediately given'.[25] Alice's biography of illness was her concrete, her data of being. 'You know that ill or well', she wrote to her friend Fanny Morse, 'one is never deprived of the power of standing for what one was meant to stand for'.[26] What mattered was not experience, or the lack of it, but impressions, how one registered and responded to experience. 'If experience consists of impressions, it may be said that impressions *are* experience', her brother Henry wrote in 1884.[27] Alice's diary reveals that she also held this belief and tried hard to be one of Henry's 'people on whom nothing is lost':[28]

> How grateful I am that I actually do *see*, to my own consciousness, the quarter of an inch that my eyes fall upon; truly, the subject is all that counts! (p. 31)

Alice's diary and letters offer evidence of the way in which she shared a language of the self with her brothers. Whilst they, however, were encouraged from childhood to confront life as spaciousness and potential, even as void,[29] making their own subjectivity both measurement and meaning, Alice was never allowed to develop the kind of psychological strength that would have made this kind of freedom tolerable. As a girl questions of philosophy and career were deemed irrelevant: her life was already determined. Ironically Henry was to ponder in his Preface to *Portrait of a Lady* whether a girl could, to use Alice's word, 'count' as a subject/Subject:

> By what process of logical accretion was this slight 'personality', the mere slim shade of an intelligent but presumptuous girl, to find itself endowed with the high attributes of a Subject? – and indeed by what thinness, at the best, would such a subject not be vitiated?[30]

Isabel Archer, the novel's heroine, can be a Subject because she is also Henry James's fictional subject. As John Goode has suggested, woman as Subject within the novel keeps being resolved into object; the narrative repeatedly leads to the frozen tableau, the picture in a frame.[31] As subject of her own experience, rather than the 'beautiful incentive'[32] for James's imagination, the choices she can make are severely circumscribed; hers is a woman's destiny where ultimately all she *can* choose is a husband and a house.[33]

Alice James, like her fictional counterpart, 'affronted her destiny' surrounded by a rhetoric of freedom, but bound as woman by social constraints and expectations, the already written text of patriarchy. 'Matrimony', she wrote to her friend Annie Ashburner, 'seems the only successful occupation that a woman can undertake.'[34] Though she goes on in the same letter to mock the view that 'women ought to stay home in a constant state of matrimonial expectation' in reality she received little encouragement to do anything else. Her father's attitude to his sons' education and upbringing might be radical and unconventional; his views on women, however, were predictably narrow and unenlightened. In 1853, five years after Alice's birth, Henry James Sr published an article, 'Woman and the Woman's Movement' in which he made plain his opposition to women's claim to equality with men:

> The very virtue of woman, her practical sense, which leaves her indifferent to past and future alike, and keeps her the busy blessing of the present hour, disqualifies her for all didactic dignity. Learning

and wisdom do not become her . . . Her aim in life is . . . simply to
love and bless man.[35]

It is a revealing statement of how woman, extolled for her 'natural'
virtue, is also imprisoned within male idealisations of her; because
she is already 'woman', she can be denied both history and
aspiration as a human Subject.

Not surprisingly Alice's education, unlike her brothers', was
given little importance within the family. Whilst they travelled and
experimented, she mostly stayed at home with a mother, Mary, who
seems to have offered, through example, a powerful reinforcement
of her father's precepts about women. A successful 'Angel in the
House' she was revered by all the family for her saintly, selfless
devotion. In 1891, three months before her own death, Alice
contemplated how, since her mother died and 'all personal claim
on her vanished'

> she has dwelt in my mind a beautiful illumined memory, the essence
> of divine maternity from which I was to learn great things, give all,
> but ask nothing. (p. 221)

It is interesting that Alice's veneration of her mother's memory is
made possible by her mother no longer being there either to meet
or frustrate her daughter's needs. Unconsciously Alice raises the
question: if the daughter, too, is taught to ask nothing, what was
the mother actually required to give? There is a similar ambiguity
about Henry's reminiscences of his mother for all his intense filial
piety and his acknowledgement of 'our constant depths of
indebtedness'. 'The only thing I might have questioned', he writes,
'was the possibility of a selflessness so consistently and unabatedly
active of its having anything ever left *acutely* to offer.'[36] An
impossible ideal of maternal selflessness undoubtedly concealed a
more complex family dynamic. As Jean Strouse suggests, Mary
James's self-sacrifice could also have been used selfishly as a
formidable weapon, a way of making everyone her debtor.[37]

Unlike her mother Alice did not marry and never had a family
of her own in which to exercise her power. Although she seems to
have been ambivalent about marriage throughout her life Alice did
not refuse to marry as a positive assertion of independence and
experienced her spinsterhood as failure.[38] 'Don't you love to
hear of successful engagements', she wrote to her friend Annie

Ashburner in 1876, 'it always sends a thrill of joy thro' me, altho' my own turn I am afraid will never come on this side of the grave.'[39] At the age of 28 she had become almost stoical about her fate, though she could not altogether conceal her sense of injustice:

> It provokes me so to see all the most insignificant women married, & not only married, but mothers of the most splendid looking children whilst the significant women are either unmarried, or if married childless.[40]

She could include herself in the general case, of course, and find a negative sense of value there. Being a 'significant woman' seemed to be at odds with being 'feminine' and though Alice did not consistently reject how society defined women she could be openly contemptuous of it. She was pleased when one friend acquired a 'feminine softness' through marriage that she had seemed to lack before;[41] another friend, however, was satirised as 'a joy to the masculine mind' because 'she is the embodiment of all their pet theories about women'.[42] 'Femininity' was a largely masculine construct she implied; it meant pleasing men, becoming a mirror of male desire. In her own case, as she wrote to William in 1886, her failure could be seen as a failure to take up this passive, 'receptive attitude' in relation to men, 'that cardinal virtue in women, the absence of which has always made me so uncharming to & uncharmed by the male sex'.[43] Lacking the 'cardinal virtue' could be weakness or strength and Alice here allows herself both positions, passive and active, rejected and rejecting.

Alice made only one attempt to find an alternative vocation to marriage whilst she lived in Cambridge. In 1875 she became a history tutor for a correspondence school for women called *The Society to Encourage Studies at Home*. Though enthusiastic about the Society she seems not to have persevered with it for long. The key to why she gave up may well be in the letters that she wrote at the time which, for all their bravado, also reveal her sensitivity to 'difference'. In 1876 she chastised her friend, Annie Ashburner, for not taking her more seriously:

> I am deeply hurt at yr. ridicule of my professorial character I assure you it is not a thing to be laughed at some day you may be only too happy to sit at my feet.[44]

Whilst seeming to express annoyance, Alice also defends herself against it through overstatement, signalling to her friend that she too can laugh at her own pretensions. The letter suggests that Alice may have found it difficult to take *herself* seriously in a role which others found odd or risible. Looking back on the period of her adolescence and early womanhood from her diary in 1890 Alice gave a sombre picture of how, lacking outlets for action or self-fulfilment, she turned her energy against herself:

> The blank youthful mind, ignorant of catastrophe, stands crushed and bewildered before the perpetual postponement of its hopes, things promised in the dawn that the sunset ne'er fulfils. Owing to muscular circumstances my youth was not of the most ardent, but I had to peg away pretty hard between 12 and 24, 'killing myself,' as some one calls it – absorbing into the bone that the better part is to clothe oneself in neutral tints, walk by still waters, and possess one's soul in silence. How I recall the low grey Newport sky in that winter of 62–3 as I used to wander about over the cliffs, my young soul struggling out of its swaddling-clothes as the knowledge crystallized within me of what Life meant for me, one simple, single and before which all mystery vanished. (p. 95)

Her period of awakening to the dullness of life occurred when she was 14; it coincided, in other words, with puberty, with her entry into womanhood and all that that implied in terms of a new, and very much more restricted, social role.[45] Alice's retrospective account of her early life with its perpetual postponement of hopes provides a bitter commentary on her father's belief that women essentially inhabit a different order of time, ahistorical time without past and future. Being outside history, refused existence in a time of 'progression and arrival', could also mean subjectively, as Alice illustrates, a dangerous identification with absence, silence and non-being.[46]

The hidden self

It is easy for us now, with the insights of psychoanalysis, to say that Alice was 'killing herself' psychically rather than physically; that her illness, in a complicated crossing and recrossing between body and mind, was the playing out across her body of the conflict, anger and pain that her female role inflicted upon her and, in the same moment of repression, forbade her to express. Her psychologically minded brother Henry also believed that Alice in some sense willed her own illness, that disablement was her way of enabling her existence. 'Her tragic health was in a manner the only solution for her of the practical problem of life' he wrote to William shortly after her death.[47] For Alice, like many other nineteenth-century women, hysterical illness was one way of responding to her intolerable plight as a woman, the conflicts and tensions of her social role; but it is obviously a highly ambivalent response. Caroll Smith-Rosenberg has described the way hysteria, viewed as illness and thus transitory and unavoidable, gained for the woman freedom from day-to-day responsibilities, sympathy and attention; these secondary compensations, however, were purchased 'only at the cost of pain, disability, and intensification of woman's traditional passivity and dependence'. 'Indeed', Rosenberg goes on to argue 'a complex interplay existed between the character traits assigned women in Victorian society and the characteristic symptoms of the nineteenth-century hysteric: dependency, fragility, emotionality, narcissism.'[48] Hysteria becomes a place where submission and resistance to female socialisation exist together and where deviant and normative identifications of woman can be seen to traverse each other.

Rosenberg's caveat that though it is possible to trace something of the function and character of hysteria in social terms, the reason why particular individuals adopted that behaviour pattern must remain obscure also applies in Alice's case: it is impossible simply to find a cause for her illness.[49] The problem of treating as representative something which by its very nature must remain hidden within the individual psyche is complicated by the way hysteria seems to unsettle the very terms in which we attempt to 'explain' it, moving between social and psychological models, body and mind, conscious and unconscious, physician and patient.

Psychoanalysis was born, of course, precisely out of the need to provide an explanation for what seemed inexplicable about hysteria. Freud and Breuer published their *Studies on Hysteria* in 1895, some three years after Alice's death, in which they developed their own way of reading and understanding the symptoms. Paradoxically psychoanalytic interpretation, as Freud recognised, depended upon finding a different meaning for interpretation itself, on science becoming implicated in the problems of creative writing and storytelling:

The fact is that local diagnosis and electrical reactions lead nowhere in the study of hysteria, whereas a detailed description of mental processes such as we are accustomed to find in the works of imaginative writers enables me, with the use of a few psychological formulas, to obtain at least some kind of insight into the course of that affection.[50]

The hysteric for Freud and Breuer was someone who could not tell the story of their lives, who, having forgotten the past, 'suffered from reminiscences'[51] and whose story was therefore incomplete, marred by gaps and hiatuses. The task of the analyst, through the medium of psychoanalytic interpretation, was to help the patient retell their story as linear narrative, to unblock memory, and thus also reinstate logical explanation for what had been uncannily like fiction.[52] 'Once we have discovered the concealed motives, which have often remained unconscious, and have taken them into account, nothing that is puzzling or contrary to rule remains in hysterical connections of thought, any more than in normal ones.'[53] But in that Freud and Breuer as scientists had first to forget themselves in order for their patients to remember, in that they must enter consciously and unconsciously through transference and counter-transference into the stories they are told, they also reveal their own potential for hysteria. It is only by mastering fiction, the fantasy of repressed desire, through the completeness of theory that they can also 'know' (by insisting on) the difference between analyst and patient, and by implication, male and female.

It is the incomplete nature of Freud's case study of Dora which has made it such an important site of feminist rereadings of Freudian theory. Though Freud did not link hysteria exclusively with women, most of his and Breuer's patients were women, and Freud went on to develop his theories specifically in terms of female sexuality. The claim to universality helps hide the extent to which the meaning of femininity is itself at issue in Freud's interpretation of Dora just as analytic discourse also conceals the extent to which he is also telling the story of his own repressed desire. Dora's resistance to Freudian analysis – she broke off the treatment before it was completed – has been reinterpreted by feminists as her refusal to occupy the position as female assigned to her under patriarchy, her refusal to be contained by a plot which makes her an object of exchange between men; similarly Freud's desire to overcome the fragmentary nature of the analysis, to insist on the totality of his own knowledge, exposes how much it is *his* story and opens it up to alternative readings, marginalised or overlooked in his effort to achieve fictional coherence. The questions which 'Dora' seems to raise by providing a place where feminine sexuality and the problematics of narrative interpretation intersect are: is hysteria Woman's story under patriarchy and is there another story that women can tell?

Alice James died too soon to encounter Freud's and Breuer's theories though her experience of hypnosis at the end of her life allowed her what amounted to a tantalising glimpse into the future.[54] She did, however, regularly seek treatment from male doctors and it is obvious from her often very amusing accounts in letters to her relatives and friends that these consultations were also highly combative, with Alice both seeking validation for herself and challenging the authority of male interpretations by speaking, through her body, a language which her doctors did not understand.[55] Alice employed metaphors of battle to describe the meetings and in 1885 she wrote to her aunt Kate about one of these 'gladiatorial encounters':[56]

> My doctor turned out as usual a *fiasco* an unprincipled one too. I could get nothing out of him & he slipped thro' my cramped & clinging grasp as skilfully as if his physical conformation had been that of an eel, instead of a Dutch cheese – The gout he looks upon as a small part of my trouble, 'it being complicated with an excessive nervous sensibility,' but I could get no suggestions of any sort as to climate, baths or diet from him. The truth was he was entirely puzzled about me & had not the manliness to say so. I got from him however a very thorough examination.

She concludes this story by blaming her own 'folly in going to a great man their *only* interest being diagnosis, & having absolutely no conscience in their way of dealing with one'.[57] Though we can hardly avoid recognising a sexual subtext to this, it would be wrong to conclude that what Alice wanted – any more than Dora – can simply be answered in terms of (hetero-) sexual repression. Again and again it is the 'intellectual degradation' of her treatment by doctors that she refers to[58] and it is as if resenting her role as senseless matter for their diagnosis or theory, she turns the situation round in her letters, picturing these 'great men' physically as unlovely or absurd and exposing them to her own linguistic skills, her gift for ridicule. In this complicated manoeuvring between physician and patient, male and female, language and body, the 'truth' as Alice suggests, may be repressed by male interpretations – by masculinity itself – which, while insisting on her inadequacy, refuses to recognise its own incompleteness and uncertainty.

Alice's brother William furnished her with a good example of how male 'health' could be posited on control of the discourse of illness. Until well into his thirties William, according to his biographer, was 'stalled in depression',[59] a psychological malaise which also manifested itself physically through recurrent psychosomatic symptoms. His later philosophical writings which advocated the overcoming of self-doubt through a conscious act of will could also be read as the enactment of this idea. In his *Varieties of Religious Experience* (1902) he writes about his own early crisis but it is also revealingly distanced by being attributed to someone else and supposedly translated from a foreign language (French). William takes up the position of sympathetic but calmly reasonable interpreter, providing the language which will make the 'other's' experience comprehensible.[60]

Earlier, in 1890, William had written about hysteria in an article he called 'The Hidden Self'. Again he is distanced, a male interpreter of the 'foreign' experience of hysteria which he links exclusively with women. Hysteria is analysed by William as a splitting within the self; using Pierre Janet as his authority he describes how 'an hysteric woman abandons part of her consciousness because she is too weak nervously to hold it all together. The abandoned part, meanwhile, may solidify into a secondary or subordinate self'.[61] Though William never seems to have acknowledged that he might also have had his sister in mind when he wrote the article, Alice in her diary applied his ideas to herself. To begin with Alice carefully praises her brother's use of the word 'abandoned'; she goes on, however, to assign it to 'his' language, 'a word commonly used by his kind' (p. 148) and seems doubtful of its application to herself: 'I have never unfortunately been able to abandon my consciousness and get five minutes' rest' (p. 149). In the remainder of the entry she uses the word repeatedly, drawing it into her own experience and making it her own; as she does so she also describes a movement of the word towards the body. 'Abandonment' becomes part of a tense struggle for her, a 'never-ending fight', whereby she deliberately 'abandons' or loses control of her body in order to gain greater control over her mind. 'So, with the rest, you abandon the pit of your stomach, the palms of your hands, the soles of your feet, and refuse to keep them sane' (p. 150). William's idea of 'splitting' becomes a fragmentation of the body, a breaking of it into parts, as Alice (hysterically) converts her 'weakness' – for William a state of mental frailty – into 'physical weakness' and lapses in 'muscular sanity'. Dissociated from weakness – rather than weakly dissociated – she keeps her mind through an almost superhuman effort of consciousness.

Two weeks later, in her next entry in her diary, she returned to the word again, indicating how deeply it had stuck in her mind. She writes jocularly that she 'must "abandon" the rhetorical part of me and forgo the eloquent peroration with which I meant to embellish the above, on the ignorant asininity of the medical profession in its treatment of nervous disorders' (p. 150). While she ironically distances herself both from her brother's term and the 'ignorant asininity' of doctors without overtly making the connection between them the sentence itself suggests an interesting conjunction. Alice rejects diagnosis and theory which situate her simply as object, to which she must 'abandon' herself as conscious subject. How William's word defines her could also be interpreted as a metaphor for her positioning within 'male' language. In her diary she both colludes with and rejects her brother's writing. Reading herself there means enacting contradictory identifications; her translation of his meaning into her 'body language' or physical symptom is not only an indication of her hysterical splitting, it also returns his word as itself parodoxical (or hysterical), a 'conscious abandonment'.

Freud's cure for hysteria – that the hysteric must tell her own story – acknowledges that what is at stake for both analyst and patient is the hysteric's problematic relation to language. What he fails to see, however, is the difficulty posed by language itself. As Claire Kahane writes: 'When his patients came into possession of their own stories, Freud believed, they would not have to speak across the body. Yet Freud neglected to ask how a woman comes into possession of her own story, becomes a subject, when every narrative convention assigns her a place as object of desire.'[62] Juliet Mitchell goes further when she sees all narratives by women as necessarily hysterical: 'I do not believe there is such a thing as female writing, a "woman's voice". There is the hysteric's voice which is *the woman's masculine language* (one has to speak "masculinely" in a phallocentric world) talking about feminine experience.'[63] Constructing the story of herself, can only, according to this view, reinscribe the problem and the hysteric comes to figure woman's inevitable splitting across the field of masculine discourse. It is one of the ironies – or necessary lessons in the multiplicity of truth – that it is Freud himself who teaches us about the shifting and divided forms of sexual and psychic identity, at the same time as seeking to contain the threat that femininity posed to his own capacity for coherent narrative. There is perhaps an instructive connection, as Mary Jacobus suggests, between the hysteric's attempt to make her body signify, to become her text, and thus deny (or forget) the alienation involved in representation and the (male) analyst's refusal to acknowledge his own lack, the gaps and silences of his interpretation.[64] Both deny the difficulty or impossibility of the female subject which nevertheless exists as a ghostly absence which haunts them both. Alice James, a hysterical autobiographer, who could and could not tell her own story, also instructs us in the hysteria of autobiography, calling forth the need for a split or divided reading. For it is the female subject, acted and unacted in her text, which intensifies our sense of destabilisation and warns us of the precariousness of any text.

'Annals of the sickroom'[65]

The story that we can tell about Alice James, piecing together her biography from her diary and letters, is not the story that Alice wished to tell about herself. Though some of the interest of her diary for a modern reader must reside in the way Alice comes to figure historically, situated as female within the circumstances, limits and repressions of her age and culture, we are also aware that she continually insists that there is more to her than the reading offered by her life. 'The only thing which survives is the resistance we bring to life and not the strain life brings to us,' she wrote in her diary, in 1890, two years before her death. Yet this statement, like so much of the diary, is fraught with ambiguity: language doubles back on Alice, supplying another meaning to her heroic assertion of resistance to life, one which has deadly implications. The problem becomes for Alice and her readers: how can she represent herself in terms of a life whose meaning she also refuses? How can we trace in her writing the 'more' denied by her biography or life history, without also reading her diary – given that in it she is also 'written by' history and discourse – as evidence of less? The argument seems to turn partly on the difference between auto-biographical and biographical forms; yet that difference, both generally and more specifically in Alice's case, is more difficult to sustain than may first appear.

This is a point taken up by John Sturrock in an article in which he laments how frequently autobiographers simply follow the model of biography, writing what he calls 'pseudobiographies' by doing no more than substituting 'I' for the 'he' or 'she' of biography. Sturrock advocates a more definite distinction between the two genres based on the writer's relationship to 'the sense of an ending'. Whilst biography 'like all narrative is teleological', for Sturrock, having as its destination 'a single, terminal point in time – the moment of the biographee's death or retirement' the telos of autobiography is different: what ultimately matters is not the subject's past achievement but the restatement of it in the present, the autobiographical act itself which forms 'a whole, unfinished series of points in time'; accordingly the autobiographer's perspective unlike the biographer's, has no obvious limits but necessarily 'grows longer as he writes'.[66]

Alice James, writing a diary, comes close to Sturrock's recommendation for a new model of autobiography, avoiding 'the deceptive continuity of narrative' by situating herself as subject in the 'intermittent' act of writing itself.[67] However as a description of the diary this will not quite do for if the record of Alice's days form a sequence without a predetermined conclusion, without the linking of causality, it is also true that, even before 'the blessed peace of the end' (p. 208) looked certain, to Alice's mind her days were already numbered. 'How amusing it is to see the fixed mosaic of one's little destiny being filled out by the tiny blocks of events', she wrote in March 1891 (p. 181); day-to-day happenings could only further confirm the pattern of a life already set out in stone. For Alice, positioning herself as reader of others' lives as well as her own, lives became fictions where 'the stamp of the ending' was also the necessary final imprint of an inevitable design (p. 151).

In her book, *Writing Beyond the Ending*, Rachel Blau DuPlessis describes the stories that nineteenth-century society can tell about women, the ideological scripts that also underpin and constrain narrative possibility, as providing a choice between marriage and death; death comes to the heroine as a punishment for transgressive desire, when 'energies of selfhood, often represented by sexuality . . . are expended outside the "couvert" of marriage or valid romance'. But death, DuPlessis argues, can also be the fate of female characters 'who cannot properly negotiate an entrance into teleological love relations, ones with appropriate ends'.[68] 'Writing beyond the ending' is DuPlessis's term for twentieth-century novelists' refusal or revision of the dominant narrative solutions to women's lives, the search beyond the limits of romance for alternative outcomes.

But what if, as was the case with Alice James, death is not just the sign of a narrative impasse but the only moment at which her life could signify? What if the 'end' makes plausible a 'fantastic' (p. 104) outpouring of symptoms, joining unaccountable effects to causes that can be recognised as 'real'? What if the sacrifice of her body to one text, the 'heroine's text'[69] of failed or unrealized (heterosexual) romance, makes possible, by the same lethal token, her access to another? By dying Alice could both live out an exemplary female fate and *at the same time* rewrite it by becoming the central actor in the drama of her own death. By closing the gap between her life and its representation – literally embodying what as female she signified – she could also open another, duplicating patriarchy's account of her with a story in which the difference lay – and herein a feminist reading must try to locate *her* difference – that she had written it herself. If Alice James found it impossible to write (or live) 'beyond the ending' in DuPlessis's terms, all she could do, as a last resort, was to try to turn the prescribed ending to her own ends.

'Pseudobiography' – the 'convenient fiction' of a chronological life story on which, according to Sturrock, so many autobiographies rely[70] – is Alice's pretext: the convention that underlies her writing and a conviction adopted in her defence. Nevertheless the diary as diary still exists within another order of time, the immediate and uncertain time of writing itself. This for Sturrock, of course, is precisely the point: the process of narration and the events narrated are not the same[71] and autobiographical writing can either attempt to deny this split by creating the fiction of a unified selfhood or, as some postmodern writers have done, deliberately expose and exploit it.[72] At another level, of course, Sturrock, whilst seeking to unmask realism, is simply giving us a more current version of the masculine universal: 'pseudo-biography' applied to Alice James's writing, because of the overlooked or repressed implications of gender, takes on an interestingly different set of resonances. Already inscribed within a female destiny which debars her from (male) subjecthood and its fictions – a diary is her chosen form, of course, partly because of this exclusion – all Alice could do was to imitate: the fictional nature of identity, we could say, was what Alice lived by; it was her only access to truth. The diary exists less as an alternative and self-conscious adventure in and with language (*pace* Sturrock) than it does through the intertextual dialogue it establishes with these other fictions. But because it is 'more' than this, not just these fictions but something else as well, it could also be seen as gesturing towards a different possibility, the 'elsewhere' of female subjectivity.

Luce Irigaray has pointed to this 'elsewhere' in a now famous passage from 'The Power of Discourse' where she describes how a woman, through what she calls 'mimesis', can deliberately play out her subordinate role within discourse 'without allowing herself to be simply reduced to it'; instead she will expose 'what was supposed to remain invisible'. 'To play with mimesis', according to Irigaray,

> also means 'to unveil' the fact the if women are such good mimics, it is because they are not simply reabsorbed in this function. *They also remain elsewhere.*[73]

The link between this strategy of 'mimesis' and hysteria, a link which Irigaray herself makes,[74] is in its recasting of the hysteric's ability to act or mime. Elizabeth Grosz has carefully drawn the parallel:

> The hysteric mimes, and thus exceeds, the patriarchal requirements of femininity. So too Irigaray mimes and thus exceeds the strategy of the hysteric.[75]

Alice James's diary is not, of course, self-consciously subversive writing. What it does do, however, is to place Alice, through writing, in an obliquely 'knowing' relation to her own hysteria. Having gained the admission from a doctor, some nine months before the diagnosis of terminal illness, that people with her 'condition' sometimes did die, she commented:

> This is most cheering to all parties – the only drawback being that it
> will probably be in my sleep so that I shall not be one of the audience,
> dreadful fraud! a creature who has been denied all dramatic episodes
> might be allowed, I think, to assist at her extinction. (p. 135)

The exclamation, 'dreadful fraud', applies at the most obvious level
to Alice's death which she imagines happening in a way which will
make her unable to witness it. However what, at another level, is
'fraudulent' about death (and Alice's writing about it) is that it is
taking the place of the 'dramatic episodes' she has already been
cheated of in life. What Alice actually desires is disallowed her: by
staging her own death in her writing – not an absence of drama but
the drama of her own absence – she also imagines how 'elsewhere'
she might be 'allowed' to be visible. Another reading of this extract
would make Alice herself the 'dreadful fraud', a hysteric who was
only allowed (by her society, by herself) to recognise herself as
performer (subject or agent) within a dialectics of performance,
thus ensuring that she could do nothing. However, as death
approached, Alice increasingly understood it in terms of a 'double'
drama in which she took both parts herself, doubling as spectator/
writer and actress. Performance as a textual pose or trope created
an imaginary space beyond what it represented; by locating Alice
in one scene what it also did was to conjure up a vision of herself
in other unlived scenes of possibility:

> Having it to look forward to for a while seems to double the value
> of the event, for one becomes suddenly picturesque to oneself, and
> one's wavering little individuality stands out with a cameo effect and
> one has the tenderest indulgence for all the abortive little *stretchings
> out* which crowd in upon the memory. (p. 208)

Performance as a motif within the diary opens up a gap or
distance from what it represents – a gap into which other
possibilities 'crowd'. Similarly Alice's sickroom also figures as a site
of ambiguity: a place of typically female limitation it becomes,
through the writing of the diary, the scene of Alice's authorship.
As we have already noted, the period of Alice's chronic invalidism
began on her return to England in 1885; by the time she started to
keep her diary in 1889 she was scarcely able to function outside her
sickroom, certainly not unaided, though during the period of the
diary's composition there were various different rooms, first in

Leamington, then in London. The last was in a house of her own with her companion Katharine Loring and was the most successful. 'We are so absurdly happy in our decidedly silly little house' she wrote in April 1891 (p. 200). Restriction is an important theme in the diary and though at times Alice found her fate absurd – 'What a grotesque I am to be sure! Lying in this room, with the resistance of a thistledown' (pp. 48–9) – she was more inclined to represent herself as stoically making the best of things:

> If I can get on to my sofa and occupy myself for four hours, at intervals, thro' the day, scribbling my notes and able to read the books that belong to me, in that they clarify the density and shape the formless mass within, Life seems inconceivably rich. (p. 113)

By referring to her diary writing casually as 'scribbling my notes' [76] and associating her reading and writing with passivity and inability, Alice would seem simply to be accepting her 'feminine' place within patriarchal discourse. Yet, it is also the case that by sanctioning the boundaries of the sickroom, Alice found a kind of sanction for herself as well. From its station on the edge, or margins, of society, she could look out; she could inscribe herself in a scene of writing at a frontier between inner and outer, domestic and public, present and past; she could also invoke possibility by gesturing towards territories which lay out of sight, beyond her own domain.

Space itself thus figures as a complex source of meaning in the diary. Alice used physical location to create a pervasive dynamic in her writing, continually mapping the geographical and national differences between England and America. In a sense Alice could be safely ill in England because she never felt she belonged there: 'It's rather strange that here, among this robust and sanguine people, I feel not the least shame or degradation at being ill, as I used at home among the anaemic and the fagged' (p. 36). Exiled from America, she was suspended emotionally in a space between. Her distance from both countries allowed her to establish a double sense of superiority: the English were 'inartistic' (p. 47) and above all 'pharisaical' and Alice mounted in her diary an eloquent indictment of the English political system and the values it supported (pp. 87–8); however Americans when thought about or encountered in England could seem blind to the virtues of English 'civility' and 'complexity' which Alice herself could both see and value (p. 33). England represented a sense of continuity through time, layers of tradition with a 'far-backness' (p. 182) very different from the American experience of being 'born to "rattle round" in space' (p. 174). English lack of expectation gave Alice a place to retreat to away from the ideology of individual freedom which defined her, in American terms, as a failure. However, the evocation, however sentimentally, by Alice of the hopeful prospects and unpopulated horizons of America introduced a different sense of space into her diary, the possibility of an imaginative expansion far beyond the confines of the sickroom:

> What a longing to see a shaft of sunshine shimmering thro' the pines, breathe in the resinous air and throw my withered body down upon my mother earth, bury my face in the coarse grass, worshipping all that the ugly, raw emptiness of the blessed land stands for – the embodiment of a Huge chance for hemmed in Humanity! (p. 119)

A similar movement between different perspectives is suggested in the way Alice responded to the people who inhabited her immediate environment to whom she frequently condescended, albeit sometimes guiltily, and the public 'others' on whom she also passed judgement as a political and historical commentator. She mentions 'my human bric-a-brac, the Bachelers' (p. 84) at one point and Alice sometimes saw herself as a collector of human specimens, noticing what was odd, funny or representative in 'ordinary' people. It was an attitude, of course, which also put her at a remove or elevated her above them. 'I wonder what part of me is fed by snubbing poor little Nurse' (p. 70) she pondered on one occasion. Indeed her Nurse was often made the butt of wry comments in her journal and physical dependency was offset by Alice affirming at her nurse's expense, her own superior intelligence and sensibility. The ironic contest between her fantasies of (male) power – she could feel herself to have 'the potency of Bismarck' (p. 48) – and a (female) physical incapacity, an 'excess of weakness' (p. 49) which made a mockery of her own mental strivings, was also a frequent scenario in her relationship with others. At the same time we could also see Alice asking by means of this constant movement of displacement where does masculinity and femininity belong – inside or outside her, inside or outside the sickroom – and consequently questioning as well where her place was within or across the boundaries of gender.

This question – a making of gender demarcation questionable – also underlies the way Alice approached the public, political arena, the masculine sphere. Excluded as participant, she nevertheless surveyed it from her sickroom with an impressive authority. Taking a strong moral and political stance, Alice was on the look out for signs of weakness lurking beneath the mask of official prestige, moments of inadequacy in the men who wielded power which thus 'domesticated' or feminised them. During the inquiry into allegations against Parnell – Alice was an ardent supporter of Irish home rule – she turned on the MP Henry Labouchère, warning him against complacency:

> Be careful Labbie! Creatures like you are only possible as long as they are successful; your moral flimsiness and the strain you put on the aesthetic sense are such that if you fail in worldly shrewdness and are led away like the hysterical, you fall like a house of cards. (p. 98)

It would be easy (and partly true) to see Alice here displacing her 'hysterical' anxieties on to the political scene, attacking others by attributing her own symptoms to them, just as she had with her doctors (and by the way revealing a connection between illness and aggression). However, something more is at stake. 'History is hysterical', Roland Barthes has written, 'it is constituted only if we consider it, only if we look at it – and in order to look at it we must be excluded from it.'[77] Alice also took up a position of observation based on exclusion: however, for Alice, to see history as 'hysterical' meant to attempt to break down divisions, to read back into it the subjectivity it had disavowed, by interpreting it through the fallible personalities on which it depended. Instead of displacing her individual pathology onto society, Alice, we could say, was attempting to pay back to society the sickness it had deposited with her. This is, of course, a very different position from Barthes' for whom the 'hysteria' of history is simply an incurable condition of the subject's relation to what is 'not present'. However, the subject that Barthes writes about is not (cannot be) genderless; it is the masculine subject which secures its position of universality and neutrality through a division which makes history (and women) hysterical.

Hysteria was 'linked to place' Freud believed.[78] The hysteric 'suffering from reminiscences' experienced time as repetition, as a collapsing of the present into the past: as time without horizon or boundary. This is simply itself to repeat, in another form, the placing of hysteria on one side of a division – now that between the categories of time and space – which structures the symbolic and the subject's access to it. Like history, when seen by Barthes as what his own identity as a 'living soul' must be outside of or separate to (it is, not incidentally, his mother's history he is referring to)[79] so place, according to this paradigm, exists outside of the (masculine) subject's enunciation of himself in time except as a point of origin or return. Where this leaves woman is figuratively, if not literally as well, immobilised in a house, exiled from her own being in time and therefore also homeless within the symbolic order.

Alice well illustrates this connection between homelessness and a lack of access to time as meaningful project in the account she gives in her diary of her psychic collapse after her parents' death. As we have already seen, Alice from puberty approached life as offering her little promise of a future. Her parents' death, instead of inaugurating the possibility of a separate life, seems to have left her in a strange place, in a house haunted by the 'ghastly' (or ghostly) otherness of her own existence.

> In those ghastly days, when I was by myself in the little house in Mt. Vernon Street, how I longed to flee in to the firemen next door and escape from the 'Alone, Alone!' that echoed thro' the house, rustled down the stairs, whispered from the walls, and confronted me, like a material presence, as I sat waiting, counting the moments as they turned themselves from today into tomorrow. (p. 45)

Time can only be experienced as a time of waiting, defining and defined by her own exclusion and superfluity.

Alice, however, also produced a somewhat different account of time in her diary: a ghostly suspension of time rather than its uncanny absence, which is well worth putting beside the previous one since it prompts the question – a question which recurs in different forms throughout our reading of Alice's diary – are there other ways of thinking about about 'women's time' than negation and absence? What might the writing of that time mean?

> I have seen so little that my memory is packed with little bits which have not been wiped out by great ones, so that it all seems like a reminiscence and as I go along the childish impressions of light and colour come crowding back into my mind and with them the expectant, which then palpitated within me, lives for a ghostly moment.

Here a time outside social time, a time when memory is everything and can thus endlessly resist the pressures of a temporal economy of arrival and closure – 'it all seems like a reminiscence' – is coded as feminine through its metaphorical associations with gestation. If nothing will happen, for the 'ghostly moment' her imagination and memory gives birth to anything still might; by imagining a time which precedes her negative place within the symbolic – her 'childish impressions of light and colour' suggest the imaginary or semiotic – Alice stands momentarily on a different (feminine) threshold of what she might still become.

'A woman has nothing to laugh about when the symbolic order collapses' Julia Kristeva has famously declared.[80] Alice, who knew well the risk and anguish of her 'scaffolding' falling (p. 56) constructed a witty diary in which she joked about the deadly seriousness of her position: to laugh or joke *about* is, of course, also to interpose language or symbol between her and the materiality of her condition; it is, in Kristeva's terms, to enter the symbolic order by means of the key provided by identification with the father, by repressing the maternal or female body. Throughout the diary Alice addresses an imagined male reader, a 'you', and by doing so in effect secures her position as subject, as 'I', by 'mastering' her own discourse. On one occasion, however, she interrogated her motives for making the sex of her fictional interlocutor male, introducing at the same time the troubling question of her own femininity: '. . . dear Inconnu (please note the sex! pale shadow of Romance still surviving in the most rejected and despised by Man)' (p. 166). Seeking artistic validation without being able to shed its entanglement with her sexuality – she moves parenthetically and awkwardly here into her sexually subordinate role – Alice, as literary daughter, must look to the power of paternal approval for her writing or, more specifically in Alice's case, that power handed on to the sons.

However, with the doubleness of everything else in the diary the apparent addressee of Alice's writing is shadowed by another. The role of Alice's beloved friend, Katharine Loring, in her life and her writing should not be left unnoticed: it is Katharine who, after Alice's death, added the final words to the diary, describing Alice's effort to 'make sentences' right up to the time of her death (p. 232). It is Katharine, too, who from December 1890 was Alice's scribe, writing the diary from Alice's dictation.[81] This not only adds an extra level of meaning to those passages in the diary after that date which pay tribute to Katharine's commitment and care – 'the story of her watchfulness, patience and untiring resource cannot be told by my feeble pen' (p. 225) – but should also make us reconsider who it is Alice is addressing. If Alice commemorates her friendship by imaginatively telling a third (male) person about it, the communication that is passing between the two women at that moment – a communication which also involves the physical handing back and forward of the book between them – may be at least as important. The argument that ensued after Alice's death between Katharine and Henry as to the diary's future, with Henry, shocked first by the discovery of its existence and then by the extent of its indiscretion with regards himself, wanting it to remain private, takes on, in this respect, a more than personal significance: James's need for secrecy also has the effect of hiding the woman from view, of controlling not only what, but also who, gets into print.[82] That Katharine won this particular contest, ensuring the diary's survival, confirms the picture of her that emerges in the diary as a woman whose robust energy could be counted on. For Alice Katharine represented potentiality: she was, Alice recorded in 1889, 'as large a joke as ever, an embodiment of the stretchable, a purely transatlantic and modern possibility' (p. 56).

To summon up Katharine at this point in our reading of the diary is not, however, to attempt to transform the text, with Katharine's help, into a female or feminist triumph over male censorship; nor is it to suggest there may be a privileged female position from which to read the diary, a different key which could unlock meanings hidden or submerged beneath a more outwardly conformist surface; it is rather to return us to the ambiguity of the writing itself and its subject – for the 'To whom is she speaking?' cannot be separated from another, more confusing, question: 'Who is speaking?' The specific meaning of this question in Alice's case should not be lost in its more general, negative formulation in post-structuralist theory: 'Does it matter who is speaking?'[83] It is against such immunity to the implications of sexual difference that Alice stages her dis-ease, as both woman and writer. However, between the 'joke' that Katharine embodied for Alice, the possibility of a humour that, in Alice's description of her, seems to stretch beyond or overflow boundaries (and which we could relate to Cixous' evocation of women's laughter as women's 'greatest strength')[84] and the laughter which can only emerge if women safely establish their subject status *within* the symbolic and language – between, in other words, the contesting of the limits of female subjectivity and its inscription within those limits – perhaps we are faced with the impossibility of deciding who finally has the last laugh.

CHAPTER THREE

Virginia Woolf: 'In the shadow of the letter "I"'

Moving from Alice James's sickroom to Virginia Woolf's 'room of one's own' may seem, in terms of its implications for women's autobiographical writing, like taking a huge leap forwards. However, Alice James's sickroom, as we have seen, doubled for her as the site of her potential authorship whilst Woolf can only imaginatively reach her room by means of a detour, by doubling back over the social and historical reality of the woman writer's exclusion, the very ground of Alice James's inhibitions. Asked famously to speak on the topic of 'women and fiction' in 1928 – the Newnham and Girton lectures which resulted in *A Room of One's Own* (1929) – Woolf decides to follow the train of thought that led her to the belief that 'a woman must have money and a room of her own if she is to write fiction'.[1] From the very outset, therefore, finding a place to begin means retracing her steps, putting herself into motion rather than taking up a settled position. 'I' becomes part of the narrative she invents, 'a convenient term for somebody who has no real being', the ghostly voice of the fourth Mary, the transgressive 'me', which she uses to name the figure of the woman in her text (p. 6).[2] However, as Peggy Kamuf has pointed out, by plotting her argument through metaphors of space Woolf is constantly being brought back to earth since these metaphors – like the room of Woolf's title – slide ambiguously between being the thing imagined and the context in which such acts of imagination must occur.[3] History, like an officious Beadle, springs to life in Woolf's text, interrupting her imaginative flow, ordering her to observe the convention of masculine prerogative and stay on the sidelines. It politely but just as effectively bars her way to the library or once inside confronts her with the evidence of masculine hostility towards her, diverting her rational inquiry into angry scribbles – 'anger had snatched my pencil while I dreamt' – returning her forcibly to a consciousness of her own gender and body: 'My heart had leapt. My cheeks had burnt. I had flushed with anger' (p. 32).

Yet if Woolf is unable to escape into a seamless text of her own, drawn back repeatedly to the scene of its making, her text also performs its own form of interruption. Rachel Bowlby has noted the significance of Woolf's first word, 'But' as a 'provocative interruption' of, or 'butting in' on, a discourse already in progress.[4] Is it that the woman, in order to speak, must first check the confident line of reasoning pursued by men? Later, when Woolf – or the narrator – takes down from the shelf a novel by a Mr A. – the anonymous first in a predictable line of male novelists – she is struck, after a chapter or two, by a shadow lying across the page:

> It was a straight dark bar, a shadow shaped something like the letter 'I'. One began dodging this way and that to catch a glimpse of the landscape behind it. Whether that was indeed a tree or a woman walking I was not quite sure. Back one was always hailed to the letter 'I'. (p. 95)

This is the same phallic 'I', we could surmise, which had already barred her own textual progress in the figure of the beadle, hailing her back to the straight and narrow path of masculine law. Now, however, it is Woolf's turn to interrupt: 'But . . . I had said "but" too often. One cannot go on saying "but". One must finish the sentence somehow, I rebuked myself. Shall I finish it, "But – I am bored!"' (p. 95). This ultimate form of readerly resistance is also, of course, a triumphant liberating of herself from the authority assumed to reside in the masculine point of view; the text of masculine self-preoccupation may after all hold little of interest for a woman. By enclosing the traditional or historical power of the male in a fiction of her own, Woolf also manages to reduce him to a shadow of himself, a textual signifier. Whilst the woman can only be glimpsed intermittently as a question at the edge of his text, in the scenario created by Woolf it is the woman who, as the embodied subject, has the power to move freely about the room, to take a book from the shelf and turn the page; who, centre stage, takes on all the privileges of the autobiographical subject.

A similar strategy is at work when Woolf invents the character of Judith Shakespeare. Confronted by the absence of women writers in an age which produced our most illustrious poet, Woolf refuses the argument about women's inferiority to reflect instead on the historical conditions of a woman's life at the time. The biography she imagines for Shakespeare's sister is tragic: suffering both external opposition and internal conflict, caught between her 'poet's heart' and her 'woman's body', she kills herself. Yet the point of this story is not simply to reinforce an absence, to condemn the woman again to a deathly silence; rather Woolf creates a narrative plausible enough to stand beside – or stand in for – the historical account; she gives literal embodiment to what had previously been unheard of – the woman who could write as well as Shakespeare. Indeed, the implications of Woolf's narrative go further: for if history is *like this* – a story which she has made up – may not historical 'truth' owe more than it acknowledges to fiction in the first place; may not the lines of division between 'history' and 'fiction' be more confused and confusing than have traditionally been allowed. Dr Johnson's misogynist dictum about women preaching is for Woolf paradigmatic of the kind of prejudice which could have assailed Judith Shakespeare in the past; she also finds the same words repeated in the present about women composing: '"Sir, a woman's composing is like a dog's walking on his hind legs. It is not done well, but you are surprised to find it done at all."' As such it becomes an example of the way 'history accurately repeats itself' (p. 53). But as Tania Modleski has pointed out, history is here *inaccurately* repeating itself, sliding between Woolf's fiction and historical fact; indeed history could be based, Woolf seems to imply, on no more than the constant repetition of male prejudice, on opinion repeated authoritatively enough and often enough to take on all the force of a truth.[5]

In effect, Woolf is only able to define her 'room of one's own' as a series of exits and entrances, through its relation to other rooms. Historically, she finds women were confined and violence towards them condoned; deprived of legal rights a wife could be beaten or a daughter 'locked up, beaten and flung about the room' (p. 42). Women's potential lies elsewhere, in a room still waiting to be entered, a 'vast chamber where nobody has yet been'. Of necessity

Woolf can imagine it only dimly: 'It is all half lights and profound shadows like those serpentine caves where one goes with a candle peering up and down, not knowing where one is stepping' (p. 80). This room, which takes on the uncanny configuration of a dream, is the space created by desire *if* the woman had a 'room of her own'; yet a 'room of one's own', the necessary material base for creativity, is also conditional on the capacity to imagine it, on its being where it has not yet been thought to be. In a sense each of these rooms forms a passage-way to the other: to situate the woman historically, materially, a space other than absence must be imagined for her; access must be sought through fiction to history, a proceeding which will also, by the way, prise open holes in the self-enclosed structure of historical truth.

Moreover, for Woolf to think of 'a room of one's own' – if we now take that in its other sense to refer to the singular, bounded, space of subjectivity – requires her to think collaboratively, not just about the collaboration of one woman with another which might come about 'if Chloe liked Olivia' (p. 80) but as if the subjectivity of any woman were unthinkable without taking into account the whole collective history of women's negation, all the 'infinitely obscure lives' that 'remain to be recorded' (p. 85). Woolf's intention can never be simply to install one subject in place of another, to substitute a feminine subject for a masculine one; rather entering *her own* internal dwelling may mean breaking down the walls of the old, stable ego, thinking not in terms of one room but many:

> One goes into the room – but the resources of the English language would be much put to the stretch, and whole flights of words would need to wing their way illegitimately into existence before a woman could say what happens when she goes into the room. The rooms differ so completely; they are calm or thunderous; open on to the sea, or, on the contrary, give on to a prison yard; are hung with washing; or alive with opals and silks; are hard as horsehair or soft as feathers – one has only to go into any room in any street for the whole of that extremely complex force of femininity to fly in one's face. How should it be otherwise? For women have sat indoors all these millions of years. (p. 83)

A feminine 'one' entering the room constitutes herself in language in a way which is as yet unthinkable; she could do so only through fantastic and transgressive flights of words.[6] Yet the room she enters can never be 'one' – she can never be represented as the unified subject of discourse and history – since her difference also resides in her multiplicity, or her forms of difference are multiple, not recuperable to one and the same.[7] Woolf holds out the hope that women are standing on the threshold of a new era; that women writers, like her imaginary Mary Carmichael, will develop forms of writing which could inscribe difference. Yet 'the complex force of femininity' – existing in the place of repression it has always occupied within history – is precisely, once acknowledged, what disrupts discourse, 'flying in the face' of all attempts to represent it. What Woolf seems to be suggesting here, anticipating the work of Julia Kristeva some fifty years later, is that feminine difference is 'above and beyond nomenclatures and ideologies'; that it cannot be defined in a discourse built upon its repression.[8] Thus it inevitably exceeds, and threatens to destroy, its own condition of representation.

In her attempt to produce a theoretical account of women and fiction in *A Room of One's Own* Woolf turns to autobiography giving us, in place of the theorist's authoritative stance, personal ramblings; yet this autobiographical mode quickly establishes that it can be no more than a fiction, the story of how difficult – if not impossible – it is for a woman to inhabit that autobiographical space.[9] Woolf's extremely subtle and provocative thinking about women's autobiographical writing seems to prefigure many of the contemporary debates about writing and sexual difference:[10] she saw the importance of autobiography for women as well as how it was inseparable from the process of its own self-questioning, from a discursive leap into the unknown. Three months before her own death, on Christmas Eve, 1940, Woolf had declared to her friend Ethel Smyth: 'There's never been a woman's autobiography.' This may seem an odd statement for someone who, over the same year, had been intensely involved in writing her own, remarkable memoir, 'A Sketch of the Past'. By this time, too, her correspondent, a prolific autobiographer, had published eight volumes of autobiographical and semi-autobiographical writing and was embarking on her ninth.[11] However, Woolf's intention was not to dismiss – nor does it seem to have been interpreted as such – but rather to encourage a more daring exploration of what could not, or had not yet, been written. She went on in the same letter:

Chastity and modesty I suppose have been the reason. Now why shouldn't you be not only the first woman to write an opera, but equally the first to tell the truths about herself? Isn't the great artist the only person to tell the truth? I should like an analysis of your sex life. As Rousseau did his. More introspection. More intimacy.[12]

As Woolf had already argued in her essay, 'Professions for Women', 'chastity and modesty', the virtues characterising the 'Angel in the House', once shed, leave the woman naked in terms of definitions of 'herself'. Having rid herself of falsehood, the woman is free to be her 'self', but that self, according to Woolf, was not easy to identify: 'Ah, but what is "herself"? I mean, what is a woman? I assure you I do not know. I do not believe that you know.'[13] 'Telling the truths' about women's sexuality and body may require something more than the risky act of self-exposure, therefore, that Woolf advocates to Smyth: it may call for a refiguring of the female body, an act not of exposing but reconstituting its significance; according to Woolf in *A Room of One's Own*, Shakespeare's sister must 'put on the body which she has so often laid down' (p. 108).

Shame and reticence were certainly strongly connected with autobiography for Woolf and, as we shall see, her inhibitions about publishing her own writing form an important motif within her career. However, it is this other need, the need to ally autobiography with experimentation, with a conscious, often playful, awareness of the self as a fiction, that I want to draw attention to here. 'All attempts to inscribe female difference within writing are a matter of inscribing women within fictions of one kind or another', Mary Jacobus has remarked in a general conclusion, following on from her discussion of Woolf's writing.[14] This is true, as we have seen, of Woolf's autobiographical narrative in *A Room of One's Own*, which pursues its subject through the by-ways of fiction. But where, we may ask, does this leave Woolf's novels? How far does their conscious experimentation connect with autobiography by their very techniques of seeming to avoid it? It could be argued that there is a way in which Woolf's undermining of realist assumptions, her foregrounding of questions of representation in her novels leads back, if not to autobiography, to an exploration of the life or lives that have not yet been written. For Woolf the question of a life and its written form – whether in biography, autobiography or fiction – were inseparable and often made her blur the boundaries of genre, disputing the authority enshrined in masculine convention. In her diary she frequently tried out labels other than 'novel' for her own fiction. Significantly it is not about *To the Lighthouse*, her most obviously autobiographical novel, but about the highly experimental *The Waves*, her 'mystical eyeless' novel[15] that she was to write: 'Autobiography it might be called' (*D*, III, p. 229). Six months earlier, she had recorded the preliminary inspiration for its writing:

> I am now and then haunted by some semi mystic very profound life of a woman, which shall all be told on one occasion; & time shall be utterly obliterated; future shall somehow blossom out of the past. (*D*, III, p. 118)

Haunted, not unlike Alice James, by some 'other', intangible meaning for a woman's life, she opens up the boundaries of the present, anticipating what has not existed in the past in the different 'potential' time of the future. A woman's life is here present to Woolf only as a glimmering absence, leading her to speculate about some different time – a time beyond the conventional boundaries of narrative time – when it can be told. Her dissolution of most of the usual markers of character and narrative in *The Waves* could well be thought of as her attempt to find a form for this elusive vision. Six years later, in a letter to Hugh Walpole, Woolf alleged that autobiography was central to her literary imagination:

> As you know, of all literature (yes, I think this is more or less true) I love autobiography most.
> In fact I sometimes think only autobiography is literature – novels are what we peel off, and come at last to the core, which is only you or me. (*L*, V, p. 142)

This 'you or me', however, which Woolf presents here as the prosaic 'core' of her writing – and which seem to replace her vision of distance with a longing for some intimate arrival – were likely to disappear if grasped directly and Woolf's modes of indirection, her quests through fiction, are also ways of refusing the fixing – and falsification – of the self.

In his study of Woolf's novels, *Virginia Woolf and the Madness of Language*, Daniel Ferrer has pointed to the continuity of all Woolf's writing, which for him is connected to the difficulty of drawing a distinction between the woman and her work:

And how could it be possible, in Virginia Woolf's case, to separate the text and what is outside it, the writing and the life? Where could we draw the line in the vast quantity of *intermediate* writings – the diary, the autobiographical fragments, the letters – which occupy such an important place in her *oeuvre* and offer many points of contact with the novels, which they often precede or double? Most critics have been aware of this impossibility of marking a boundary in the continuum which goes from the life to the diary or letters, from the diary to the autobiographical writings; from the autobiographical writings to a novel presented as autobiographical like *To the Lighthouse*; and thence to all the other novels and short stories.[16]

The degree of overlap in Woolf's writing – the way in which one text gets drawn into another – would seem to direct us back to some common point of origin in the writer's 'self'. Yet Woolf's writing consistently undermines any such transcendent or 'masterful' position for the authorial subject; it engages, rather, in a *search* for its own origins, tracking the subject through the process of writing itself.[17] Indeed as Sue Roe has pointed out, '"the history of Virginia Woolf"' was, during her lifetime, at least, a shrouded and unwritten story.'[18] According to Roe, the disjunctions between the different viewpoints Woolf employed in her writing, or the sense of some ineffable meaning which is 'screened' or withheld, could well be seen, therefore, as the best, if not the only, means of telling such a story.[19]

In what follows I will look at two of Woolf's 'intermediate' forms of writing: her diary and her unpublished memoirs. What emerges is very much a 'subject-in-process', to borrow Kristeva's useful term, a subject constructing herself through a writing which aims consistently and courageously towards the unknown. Within this writing images of space recur: perhaps not surprisingly since for Woolf to attempt to construct a female subject was to encounter space, the space of absence or the as yet unthought of space in which this subject could appear.

'Traveller's notes'[20]

The diary which Woolf kept almost without interruption during her adult life extends with an uncanny precision between the wars; begun in January 1915 the last entry she made, days before her death, was in March 1941. Poignantly, both the beginning and the end of her diary share a similar concern: amidst the record of day-to-day happenings there lurks an awareness of danger; the threat from a plane that flies overhead, or an expected air raid. 'It's odd how near the guns have got to our private life again', she wrote in 1936 (*D*, V, p. 17). Her fear, justifiably intense towards the end of her life, was that the public world in its most brutal and uncontrollable form would finally invade the private one.[21] Unpublished during her lifetime and never unequivocally destined for publication, her diary has an obvious relationship with privacy; but, the dichotomy between psyche and history for Woolf was never absolute, nor could her diary simply act as a sanctuary, a shelter for the withdrawn, private self. 'External events also have their importance', she wrote about De Quincey's autobiography, whilst recognising the innovative nature of his inwardness (*CE*, IV, p. 6). This statement could have an equal relevance for her own writing. The diary bears witness to an intricate relationship between private and public; it articulates a boundary which is never fixed, which often, indeed, painfully dissolves; which is fluid, indeterminate, a process of continual reformation.

The five volumes of Woolf's diaries published in 1978 did not include the six earlier diaries that Woolf wrote between 1897 and 1909. These, though more sporadic and tentative, do, however, suggest an important relationship to the later ones: they reveal how early and how fundamental was her sense of the intermingling of writing and identity, of the way states of self-dispersal and disunity could become the very condition out of which she, as a writer, could create pattern and wholeness. In 1908, on holiday in Italy with her sister Vanessa and her brother-in-law Clive, she differentiated her art from that of the painter (and herself from her travelling companions?) on the ground that writing was a process, a movement through conflict, following the 'flight of the mind':

> I attain a different kind of beauty, achieve a symmetry by means of infinite discords, showing all the traces of the mind's passage through the world; achieve in the end, some kind of whole made of shivering fragments; to me this seems the natural process; the flight of the mind.[22]

Woolf here, for the first time, articulates images which were central to her imaginative process and which she repeated throughout her career. However, the most interesting of these early diaries is undoubtedly the 'Cornwall Diary' which she kept between 11 August and 14 September 1905. Structured around a return – for Woolf the most important of all returns – a return to St Ives, the place of her most intense childhood memories, it hovers between familiarity and strangeness, as she attempts to relate the 'then' of her memory to 'now':

> Many were the summers we had spent in St Ives; was it not reasonable to believe that as far away we cherished the memory of them, so here on the spot where we left them we should be able to recover something tangible of their substance?
>
> Ah, how strange it was, then, to watch the familiar shapes of land & sea unroll themselves once more, as though a magician's hand had raised the curtains that hung between us, & to see once more the silent but palpable forms, which for more than ten years we had seen only in dreams or in the visions of waking hours.[23]

Towards the end of her life, thinking again about her childhood, Woolf wrote: 'It would be interesting to make the two people, I now, I then, come out in contrast.'[24] The aim is to define and limit the self by providing a negative, an 'other' as background. But, since the other is not only 'other' but also self, there is also a way in which the contrast provides a space in which to suspend the subject, estranged and altered through time, between two points. Similarly the 'Cornwall Diary' seems to destabilise memory by situating it somewhere between subjectivity, the internal shadows and dreams, and the 'palpable' forms of the landscape. Thus neither category of perception, neither inner nor outer, dissolves completely into the other and past and present neither merge nor are wholly distinct. This foreshadows the themes of Woolf's fictional return to Cornwall and her childhood in *To the Lighthouse* where the narrative inserts itself into the space between subject and object, past and present, holding it open, suggesting that their relationship is a process which dissolves and renews itself rather than a fixed abstraction. The early diary provides a prelude to her most serious and insistent concerns as a writer but it also helps to demonstrate how, in writing, Woolf was all the time repeating and remaking herself; how she embodied in the patterns and structures of her writing and not only its content, the processes and relationships which determined her own knowledge of herself as a subject.

It was in 1915, by this time a writer, awaiting publication of her first novel, *The Voyage Out*, that a diary became the necessary accompaniment of all Woolf's other more formal writing of fiction and essays. But, as Lyndall Gordon has remarked, her diary is not simply a 'writer's diary', as Leonard called the extracts that he published in 1953,[25] though it is clearly, in its often intense meditations on its own process, the diary of a writer. Significantly, however, her diary is wide-ranging and indiscriminate; it touches all the concerns of her life: her friends, acquaintances, parties, clothes, servants, holidays, outings, walks and maintains, however inward-turning it becomes, many different perspectives and sources of interest. The abundance of external reference is particularly important when we think about the gaps in this remarkably sustained document: the gap between 1915 and 1917 when she experiences a breakdown and the shorter gaps of illness and depressive withdrawal when she could not write at all. Her 'soul' was never intended by Woolf to provide the main focus for her diary and she implicitly distinguished between her writing and the record of spiritual crises, of confession and self-examination which she found in other diaries. The 'soul' in any case, according to Woolf, had a tendency to disappear when looked at directly, could not be separated from 'life', the immediate experience of movement and ephemerality which kept 'breaking in' (*D*, II, p. 234). The gaps in her diary, the 'dark underworld' which she refers to as claiming her at these times of silence (*D*, II, p. 126). and which she perhaps only explored when she could do so indirectly in fiction, tell us that writing was both concealment as well as exposure, a 'disguise', a surface which she also felt she could sink beneath. 'Directly I stop working I feel that I am sinking down, down. And as usual, I feel that if I sink further I shall reach the truth', she wrote in 1929 (*D*, III, p. 235). It is impossible to think about the diary as a record of the self since the self cannot always be recorded; rather it is a way of maintaining her life in language, of being 'in language', of creating a sensitised surface which could move or flow between visible and hidden, open and closed. It could be both a film or a facade, or alternately a bridge outwards into the world, a threshold towards which the subject was always moving. The diary, like an open door, could gesture beyond itself into the external world: 'I feel on the verge of some strenuous adventure: yes; as if this spring day were the hatching; the portal;

the opening though which I shall go upon this experience' (*D*, III, p. 219).

The keeping of a diary was closely bound up with Woolf's complex response to time. In January 1929, exploring her own feelings of ambivalence, she wrote:

> Now is life very solid, or very shifting? I am haunted by the two contradictions. This has gone on for ever: will last for ever; goes down to the bottom of the world – this moment I stand on. Also it is transitory, flying, diaphanous. I shall pass like a cloud on the waves. Perhaps it may be that though we change; one flying after another, so quick so quick, yet we are somehow successive, & continuous – we human beings; & show the light though. But what is the light? I am impressed by the transitoriness of human life to such an extent that I am often saying a farewell – after dining with Roger for instance; or reckoning how many more times I shall see Nessa. (*D*, III, p.18)

How does one relate, Woolf asks here and implicitly in all her work, the experience of substantiality and significance, the full presence of the moment, lived in the solidity of the body, to the perception of the moment's perpetual vanishing and the knowledge of a relatively imminent death? The writing of her diary was one answer to feelings of evanescence and her sense of the pressure of time is apparent at its inception – the first entry is on 1 January 1915 – and in the way she goes on drawing particular attention to the beginnings of years. By noticing the dates and years and writing them down, passing time could seemingly be held within the formal gauge of writing. In 1919, asking herself 'why she did it', that is went on writing her diary, the answer she gives herself is 'my old sense of the race of time' (*D*, I, p. 304). 'Lapses' in the writing of her diary – and she could berate herself for breaks of just a few days – become expressive of time that has been 'wasted'. 'What a disgraceful lapse!' she had written earlier in the same year, 'nothing added to my disquisition, & life allowed to waste like a tap left running. Eleven days unrecorded' (*D*, I, p. 239). To record and make conscious in her diary was also, like all her writing, an attempt to rescue the moment from the flux of experience, to make life stand still. 'Why do I trouble to be so particular with facts?', she wrote; 'I think it is my sense of the flight of time. I feel time racing like a film. I try to stop it. I prod it with my pen. I try to pin it down' (*D*,

II, p. 158). Within writing and the concentration which it required she also felt she could inhabit a place where time ceased to oppress her, a state of mind rather than a sense of achievement, which raised her above her customary preoccupation with time and loss, what she called, noting her recovery after her friend, Roger Fry's death, 'the exalted sense of being above time & death which comes from being again in a writing mood' (*D*, IV, p. 245).

But the transcendence which the diary could offer as writing is also at odds with our other sense of it as process; turning the page it all has to be done again, and Woolf, however much she attempts to elevate herself above it, is back contemplating the literal moment and a sense of ongoing time. In this way her diary seems to set out the terms of an unending struggle: it is both 'solid and shifting', its form continually acted upon, dissolved, as it 'nets' thoughts and reflections and extends the moment into significance; incapable of closure, it yet carries within itself the inescapable premonition of death. Put in another way, within her diary Woolf could both affirm consciousness and question its centrality, experiencing its collapse again and again into what encompassed it, the stream or the flux of life.

The attempt to pin experience down through writing was therefore only ever half the story for Virginia Woolf; escaping from 'the fixing properties of event and plot' (*D*, III, p. 189), or in Gillian Beer's phrase, 'slipping the burden of narrative',[26] was not only a way out of restriction for Woolf, it was also a way into unknown lives, the unplotted alternatives. Significantly, her diary seems to have helped her to develop a form which did not falsely impose a predetermined pattern upon the random and inchoate nature of experience. Early on, assessing the way in which writing her diary had increased her facility and her confidence she went on to comment in a famous passage:

> There looms ahead of me the shadow of some kind of form which a diary might attain to. I might in the course of time learn what it is that one can make of this loose, drifting material of life; finding another use for it than the use I put it to, so much more consciously and scrupulously, in fiction. What sort of diary should I like mine to be? Something loose knit, & yet not slovenly, so elastic that it will embrace any thing, solemn, slight or beautiful that comes into my mind. I should like it to resemble some deep old desk, or capacious hold-all, in which one flings a mass of odds & ends without looking

them through. I should like to come back, after a year or two, & find that the collection had sorted itself & refined itself & coalesced, as such deposits so mysteriously do, into a mould, transparent enough to reflect the light of our life, & yet steady, tranquil, composed with the aloofness of a work of art (*D*, I, p. 266).

The image of a desk seems to take us back to the idea of 'a room of one's own' in its description of a bounded yet autonomous space for the self. Yet the image is as ambivalent and multilayered as it is in her essay: as she explores it horizons open up, a depth or interiority which is boundless. The diary's formlessness, its lack of continuity, its random breaks and joining up of different moments and areas of experience – its denial of narrative – provides the most appropriate form for a shifting, questing, subjectivity. The form remains potential – 'there looms ahead of me' – present and yet also absent, 'a shadow'. It is a container, a 'mould', which is also not there, 'invisible'. This is an image which Woolf repeats the next year when she reports an important conversation with Katherine Mansfield: 'I said how my own character seemed to cut out a shape like a shadow in front of me' (*D*, II, p. 61).

Her diary could present itself to Woolf as an equally passive form of writing. She often suggested that 'it did not count as writing' (*D*, II, p. 179), that in it she could practise writing without a sense of finality. Mostly she wrote her diary after her day's work and her more strenuous engagement with language in her fiction and essays. Often it was written at tea-time, quickly, in the moments between work and seeing people, in the space between private and public worlds. Sometimes she wrote it when she could not work in any other way, unsettled by the move between houses, or by the visit of friends. 'Back from Rodmell', she wrote in 1923, 'unable to settle in; therefore I write diary. How often I have said this. An odd psychological fact that I can write when I'm too jangled to read' (*D*, II, p. 276). Occasionally she simply sought relief in it from the pressure or problems of her other writing, writing then in the morning, time usually hoarded for more intense work. In 1925 confessing in her diary that it was morning and she was not working she wrote: 'I cant settle in, contract, & shut myself off' (*D*, III, p. 29). The diary, as we have seen, was more fluid or porous than her other writing; occupying an ambivalent position as not writing it could give her a 'platform' from which to see her writing, but it could also open into her social life. The 'fidgeting' that the diary became associated with could be viewed both positively and negatively: positively it was a form of improvisation, and she was like a pianist 'with hands rambling over the piano' (*D*, III, p. 37), occupied in a kind of 'aimless searching and discovery of space', 'uncramping'[27] her mind by using the 'irresponsible' page of the diary;[28] negatively it registered her aimlessness, a nervous clutching at words, a writing towards the calm purpose that writing could offer: 'I am writing down the fidgets, so no matter if I write nonsense. I know this room too well – this view too well – I am getting it all out of focus because I cant walk through it' (*D*, II, p. 134).

The status of being 'between' – between places, between writing and sociability, between different kinds of concentration – offers, I think, an important way of understanding Woolf's diary and its significance for her both emotionally and creatively. Writing about his own unsuccessful attempts to keep a journal Roland Barthes suggested that his dissatisfaction with the form arose from the fact that the journal never really achieves the status of a text; rather it is 'the Text's limbo, its unconstituted, unevolved, and immature form'.[29] According to Barthes, the journal, taking the author rather than the world as subject, cannot escape from his egotism; it therefore disappoints, diminishing meaning, unable to 'recuperate' the word, free it from its author and release it into the 'multi-dimensional space' of a text.[30]

From a different point of view, however – from the writer's rather than the reader's – the idea of being in a state of limbo or in a 'neutral zone' could be seen as offering certain advantages. If the journal never really splits off from its reader to become other or a 'text' in Barthes' terms, the ambivalent merging between writer and writing means that both can exist in a state of potentiality. The idea of 'a neutral zone' is the psychoanalyst D.W. Winnicott's and he used it in his book *Playing and Reality* to describe 'the place' where creativity occurs; for him the creative roots of the self come from a 'desultory formless functioning' where an unintegrated state of the personality can appear, becoming organised into the personality only if reflected back.[31] This again is very suggestive when specifically applied to the writing of a diary and the way its formlessness can be experienced not as chaos but as a state preceding a sense of integration and form. It is also important that these ideas extend ambivalently both to the personality and to the writing: the 'I' merging with the body of the text can be fragmented or fluid; the writing, bound to the 'I', resists the independence of a text; their symbiosis is necessary to hold both in a state of suspension.

Woolf recorded in her diary in 1935, feeling at that moment that all desire to write had left her, that it was not the writing simply but 'the architecting that strains'; 'I cannot curve my mind to the line of a book' (*D*, V, p. 306). Earlier, in 1930, working on *The Waves* she also referred to 'this hideous shaping and moulding' (*D*, III, p. 301). In some ways her diary, occupying a different kind of space, offered her relief from the distance and perspective – the separateness – which this aspect of her writing required. Her diary could be submerged and secret, like her relationships with women;[32] it could effect a state of merging between subject and writing which is reminiscent, in psychological terms, of the pre-oedipal or the maternal. In her book, *On Not Being Able To Paint*, where she scrutinises her own relationship to the creative process, Marion Milner describes the psychodynamic tensions at work when beginning a painting:

> At the moment of having to realise the limits of the body, when beginning to make marks on the paper, all the anxieties about separation and losing what one loved could come flooding in.[33]

For Milner the important discovery is of an interchange or dialogue between inner and outer, idea and action; the realisation that the separateness of idea and reality must be enfolded again in a deeper relationship:

> One has temporarily to undo that separation of self and other which one had so laboriously achieved . . . But to do this and yet maintain one's own integrity, never to go wholly over to the opponent's side, nor yet retreat into armour-plated assertion of one's own view-point that is the task demanded. To be able to break down the barrier of space between self and other, yet at the same time to be able to maintain it, this seems to be the paradox of creativity.[34]

Milner describes the creative process here in terms of being beckoned to an edge, towards a dissolution of boundaries – and of dependence on the maternal body – which precedes identity; however the achievement of identity – reproduced in the movement away from the imaginary into a system of signs[35] – brings with it, as acknowledged above, a sense of loss. The 'paradox of creativity' could be described as the dialogue, or continual oscillation, between these states.

Woolf experienced an extreme sense of separation or loss when her writing became text, when it was first of all subjected to the detached gaze of the reader. The publication of her novels marked times of particular emotional and psychological risk for her; her anxiety as she awaited the reactions of reviewers and friends could reach an extreme pitch, often resulting in periods of depression and illness. Before the publication of what was to be her most immediately successful and acclaimed novel to date, *The Waves*, she described herself as 'trembling under the sense of complete failure' (*D*, IV, p. 43). Critical acceptance and praise brought relief and sometimes rapture – the very day after the above comment was written, having received an enthusiastic response, she notes that she 'cant write for pleasure' (*D*, IV, p. 44) – but it could also increase her longing to escape. Gradually in her diary she detaches both *The Waves* and herself from the praise it had generated. 'The W. is not what they say' she writes; and 'if The W. is anything it is an adventure which I go on alone' (*D*, IV, p. 47). These anxieties remained a constant feature of her career, unrelieved by success, seemingly going beyond a need for the confirmation of her genius by others. Again and again she expressed the desire to be through the 'splash' of publication, resisting the public persona which fame conferred on her, wanting to be submerged again, out of sight in her writing: 'I want to be through the splash & swimming in calm water again. I want to be writing unobserved' (*D*, II, p. 207). The conflict and guilt which she experienced could only be mitigated through a process of splitting, by relegating her public self to the realms of unreality and withdrawing into privacy:

> Happily, for my health of soul, I am now very little noticed, & so can forget the fictitious self, for it is half so, which fame makes up for one: I can see my famous self tapering about the world. I am more comfortable when shut up, self-contained as now. (*D*, III, p. 222)

Fame was alienating, it created a false self; but it was also a temptation to be repressed and resisted. In 1933 she wrote in her diary, triumphing over her need to notice the reviews: 'I think I've got rid of vanity: of Virginia . . . Then I need not be that self. Then I can be entirely private' (*D*, IV, p. 191).

'That self' which she also called 'that quivering bag of nerves',[36] in other words the split-off anxiety induced by public exposure, is evidence of how deeply Woolf was caught within the woman writer's double-bind; that social and psychic structuring which made her unable, as a woman, to integrate herself with the striving and public achievement which society has reserved for men. 'Fame' and 'vanity' were countered by Woolf with self-denial and renunciation, qualities traditionally cultivated by the domestic 'angel'. Within this paradigm of separate spheres Woolf can only enter the public world at the risk of forfeiting a more deeply held identity.

But the need to be always 'elsewhere', the refusal to be 'stamped and stereotyped', to be fixed in an identity, was always, in a more positive way, Woolf's response to difference, a continual revision of herself as 'known' either in terms of a (male) culturally constructed subjecthood or the object-status of woman. Egotism, whenever she encountered it either in herself or in others, was attacked mercilessly, suggesting a deep anxiety and ambivalence about an unacceptably 'aggressive' selfhood. But her rejection of egotism was also set out in more positive terms as a desire for something richer and more all-embracing. In what has become a famous reference to two of her contemporaries, Woolf wrote in her diary in 1920:

> I suppose the danger is the damned egotistical self; which ruins Joyce and (Dorothy) Richardson to my mind: is one pliant & rich enough to provide a wall for the book from oneself without its becoming, as in Joyce & Richardson, narrowing and restricting? (*D*, II, p. 14)

The combination of the idea of pliancy or movement with the hardness and rigidity we associate with a 'wall' is suggestive of that bringing together of flux and form which we can find in all Woolf's writings. It is also important that the 'wall', like the image of the desk I looked at earlier, provides structure without creating boundaries; it does not wall in or wall off. It is worth comparing this with Luce Irigaray's attempts to relate Woman to a new notion of form or formlessness, what she calls 'volume without contours'. She writes: 'This incompleteness of her form, her morphology, allows her to become something else at any moment.' Like Irigaray, Woolf here also seems to be imagining a form which corresponds to the female subject's incompleteness, her state of being 'not yet': a form without 'telos', or closure, 'neither open nor closed'.[37]

As unpublished writing, the diary could be said to occupy woman's sphere of the private and the non-social; in her diary Woolf could examine the anxiety of publication without having to confront it, finding there the restful assurance that she could return to the continuity of a private self, unharassed and unviolated by publicity. But if there is an oscillation between the diary and her other writing there is also an important oscillation within the diary itself. It creates for her that place without walls: a subjectivity, in Irigaray's terms, without closure or completeness. Often Woolf positioned herself within the diary as the reader of her own text, imagining herself surveying, retrospectively, what she had written. In March 1920 the thought of herself at 50, rereading the diary, became an encouragement to go on: 'I fancy old Virginia, putting on her spectacles to read of March 1920 will decidedly wish me to continue. Greetings! my dear ghost' (*D*, II, p. 24). 'Old Virginia' could also be a serious, censorious figure providing a perspective on the diary's shortcomings: 'Old Virginia will be ashamed to think what a chatter-box she was, always talking about people, never about politics' (*D*, II, p. 92). Similarly the future project of writing her memoirs sometimes provided Woolf with a purpose for the diary: any ephemeral note could perhaps be alchemised into a 'tiny ingot' later (*D*, V, p. 269). On other occasions, she took a half mocking view of those memoirs, using the diary to offer to the future a sense of unending contingency and 'caprice':

> But undoubtedly this diary is established & I sometimes look at it & wonder what on earth will be the fate of it. It is to serve the purpose of my memoirs. At 60 I am to sit down & write my life. As rough material for that masterpiece – & knowing the caprice of my own brain as record reader for I never know what will take my fancy, I here record that I come in to find the following letters waiting for me. (*D*, III, p. 58)

The list of letters which follows encompass both her public and private selves; their arbitrariness and the plurality of selves they address offer their own silent comment on the 'masterpiece' of a life.

The, diary reread, could take on for Woolf 'a face of its own', a face which, by implication differed from hers (*D*, I, p. 317). Yet the alienation and splitting involved in this reflective processs never called up the negative reactions which Woolf elsewhere recorded towards mirrors and photographs.[38] This may seem an obvious point since, throughout this chapter, we have seen how, in writing, Woolf was continually attempting to create multiple, shifting, reflections which could escape the fixing of identity in one position or image. 'Old Virginia', could cast many different glances on her younger self; as a future reader her interpretations of the diary were at best unpredictable. So with the idea of her memoirs, too: they could never fulfil the diary's other functions of mobility and ephemerality. However, those other 'specular' moments remind us too of the inevitability of, and *need for*, reflection in the process of identification; of the role of reflection in providing borders and separations which 'make' the subject and the work of art; and of the way the subject *becomes* his/her image, consituted in socially and culturally recognisable ways. The face of the diary – a word which perhaps recalls what we described earlier, the maternal or the loving reflection of the mother's gaze – was Woolf's attempt to create a different kind of reflection. By avoiding publication, she could also hope to circumvent some of the negative implications of the woman's social and cultural inscription. The idea of that pre-oedipal or pre-linguistic gaze of the mother is an important point of exploration in Woolf's memoirs as we shall see, focusing her nostalgia for a completeness that has been lost. However, the diary is less an act of nostalgia and recuperation than it is an attempt to have it both ways – an endless suspension of self in an act of becoming: both self *and* other, form *and* formlessness, open *and* closed. Having no determinable limits or completeness, however, as Irigaray says, does not mean that 'she is (n)ever unambiguously anything'.[39] 'I have composed myself, momentarily, by reading through this years diary', Woolf wrote in 1939. 'Thats a use for it then. It composes' (*D*,V, p. 227).

'Often it is connected with the sea & St Ives'[40]

Her diary provided Virginia Woolf with a place where she could set out a complex network of relationships between her 'self' and writing, where she could both enmesh and unravel herself. Its provisionality was an important part of its meaning for her, allowing her to exist within a kind of restlessness. 'I enjoy almost everything. Yet I have some restless searcher in me', she wrote in 1926 (*D*, III, p. 62). From within the diary she looked forward to a larger and more stable attempt to memorialise the self. At the same time, wary of fixity, she never wrote the definitive life she looked forward to but instead a series of sketches, written at different times for different audiences, and inevitably also embodying different perspectives and tones. Two of these, the early 'Reminiscences', 1908, and her last brilliant memoir, 'A Sketch of the Past', written shortly before her death, are unfinished and we owe their existence as 'texts' at all to skilful editing.[41] We can speculate that the unfinished nature of this writing has something again to do with her unresolved tensions about public exposure. 'I'm uneasy at taking this role in the public eye – afraid of autobiography in public', she wrote about *Three Guineas* in 1938, just a year before she began 'A Sketch of the Past' (*D*, V, p. 141). These fears must have complicated, if not completely prohibited, the publication of even more overt autobiographical writing.

Three of the sketches collected together in *Moments of Being* did have an audience, however. They were read to the Memoir Club, a small gathering of Bloomsbury friends which met periodically to listen to each other's personal memoirs. However, even this friendly and relatively private occasion and the, in some way, guarded nature of the writing she read there, could leave her feeling raw and anxious. After one reading she compared her 'subjective' style unfavourably with Leonard's 'objective' one, castigating herself for having written 'egotistic sentimental trash'. She goes on to voice a suspicion, however, that her discomfort could reflect a discomfort among the men in the audience, that somehow for them she was going too far:

> I couldn't help figuring a kind of uncomfortable boredom on the part of the males; to whose genial cheerful sense my revelations were at once mawkish & distasteful. (*D*, II, p. 26)

This 'genial cheerful sense', the clubbable complacency of liberal males about the unambiguous nature of truth and identity, was increasingly questioned and undermined by Virginia Woolf's own writing practice. In July 1922 – again the occasion was a meeting of the Memoir Club – she included this observation in her diary:

Lytton and Morgan read; & our standard is such that little is left for
me to hint and guess at. They say what they mean, very brilliantly;
& leave the dark as it was before. (*D*, II, p. 178)

Like the Edwardian novelists whom Virginia Woolf notoriously
attacked for their materialism – their representation of reality as
unproblematic surface[42] – here Lytton Strachey and E.M. Forster
seem similarly to be situating autobiography within certain 'known'
limits. 'Saying what you mean' depends upon an idea of the subject
as the source of meaning, a unified subject undisturbed by the only
guessable dark of the unconscious. In essays like 'De Quincey's
Autobiography' and 'The New Biography' Virginia Woolf attempted to chart a transition in the writing of autobiography and
biography – and by doing so to develop a context for her own writing
– by pointing to a new recognition of an unknown 'inner life' which
'meanders darkly and obscurely through the hidden channels of the
soul', 'deeper and more hidden emotions' which cannot be
encompassed in the conventional recording of actions and events
which make up the history of the external life (*CE*, IV, p. 230).
Acknowledging the unconscious in this way also means that the
biographer confronts what is absent or unrepresentable in a life,
that truth becomes indecipherable, inseparable from fiction. Just as
the historian can only remedy the insufficiency and partiality of facts
through fiction (and so find the overlooked and forgotten woman)
so the biographer must also turn inwards, become as well
autobiographer. 'Granite and rainbow', the images Virginia Woolf
used to suggest the biographer's impossible bringing together of
'truth' and 'person' (*CE*, IV, p. 229), also suggest the space in which
an assumed solidity of fact must establish itself, an elusive arch, a
'halo of consciousness' which curves around the act or event and
also breaks apart their continuity, the 'smooth narrative', suggesting other depths or horizons, 'arch beyond arch' (*CE*, IV, pp. 6–7).

Woolf's attention to changes in the historical development of
biography and autobiography as forms also offer a perspective on
her own career as autobiographer. Her critique was part of her own
most successful autobiographical sketch, 'A Sketch of the Past',
marking out boundaries and a beyond which could release her own
experimentation, the possibility of writing otherwise. In an earlier
memoir, 'Reminiscences', however, she followed family tradition.
By addressing the memoir to her sister Vanessa's first child, Julian,

she both gave it a meaning as tradition – the handing on of family memory from one generation to the next – and established it within tradition, taking her form from that adopted by her father in his *Mausoleum Book*, the private memoirs of his two marriages which Leslie Stephen wrote in the weeks immediately following the death of Julia and which he addressed to her children in an attempt to come to terms with her death and perhaps also the prospect of his own.[43] What Stephen told his friend Charles Eliot Norton seems to confirm this interpretation: to him he wrote that through this writing he would leave the children 'a little treasure to read for themselves when I have become a memory too'.[44]

As Christopher Dahl has pointed out, Leslie Stephen's memoir, so strongly influential for his daughter, was itself part of a larger heritage of autobiographical writing within the Stephen family which stretches back to Virginia Woolf's great grandfather, James Stephen.[45] He wrote Memoirs in the 1820s for 'the use of his children' with the idea of passing on not only his experience to the next generation but also the pious lesson to be learned from it. This linking of personal memory to family memory is paternal both in fact and implication: by writing about the past the Stephens promoted their interpretation for the future, allaying personal anxiety by finding authority and meaning (authority as meaning) in the sense of a family lineage. Though it seems to have been her avowed aim in *Reminiscences* to emulate this tradition, Virginia Woolf can only as a woman situate herself awkwardly within it. Tension about her position as woman within the family leads to another tension within the memoir: a difficulty about finding a place from which to speak.

In some ways memory could be equated with written record for Virginia Woolf and in taking on the role of family historian she turned naturally to her father's memoir for material. Both her 'monumental' rendering of Julia and her view of her mother's severe treatment of Stella – Stephen uses the word 'stern' (p. 59) – seem to be significantly influenced by her father's account. Here, for instance, is Stephen's description of Julia:

> It was just the perfect balance, the harmony of mind and body which made me feel when I looked at her the kind of pleasure which I suppose a keen artistic sense to derive from a masterpiece of Greek sculpture. It was the complete reconcilation and fulfilment of all conditions of feminine beauty. (p. 32)

Virginia Woolf also uses this analogy with Greek sculpture about her mother (p. 49), similarly emphasising her dignity and perfection: 'Her presence was large & austere, bringing with it not only joy and life, exquisite fleeting femininities, but the majesty of a nobly composed human being' (p. 41). It is noteworthy that feminine beauty is only a fleeting moment within a larger sense of her mother's humanity for Virginia Woolf; nevertheless she, like Stephen, seems to make the mother the object of a contemplative (male) gaze. Visualised within general categories which make her harmonise with, or reflect the writer, the mother, silent and unmoving, is quite literally turned into stone.

Significantly, immediately after the description quoted above, Virginia Woolf tried to undo the effect of her own writing:

> Written words of a person who is dead or still alive tend most unfortunately to drape themselves in smooth folds annulling all evidence of life. You will not find in what I say, or again in those sincere but conventional phrases in the life of your grandfather, or in the noble lamentations with which he fills the pages of his autobiography, any semblance of a woman whom you can love (pp. 41–2).

Taking up a position with her father – seeing her writing as similar to his – Virginia Woolf is at the same time aware that her mother remains hidden behind the words, on the other side of a division, her living spirit obscured by the deathly shroud of language. Her mother's language, unlike her father's is unrecorded, unwritten. Virginia Woolf tries to capture it as a series of elusive gestures, traces of words rather than meaningful speech, moments contained within a ceaseless flow of movement. The problem for Virginia Woolf – though not yet a fully worked out problematic within her writing – is how to make her mother memorable within a discourse which emphasises significance rather than spontaneity, from which her mother as subject, rather than object, is missing.

In *Reminiscences* Woolf traces the relationship between her father and mother and the daughters, Stella and then Vanessa, who, after her death, took her place within the family. Each is associated with silence and must face the demands of the father, noisily and insistently articulated. First his expression of grief overwhelms 'a true and most vivid mother' (p. 53): 'tears and groans, reproaches and protestations of affection, high talk of duty and work and living for others' (p. 52). Stella, who returns from holiday to her mother's deathbed 'with a consciousness like that of some tormented dumb animal' (p. 50) is unable to meet Stephen intellectually and is expected because of her 'feminine' nature to offer up her independence to him. Vanessa, his next 'victim' (p. 65) becomes, after Stella's death, the recipient of his 'intolerable speeches'. The memoir ends with Vanessa's silence, not as a stony reponse to the father but to Virginia's jealous complaints about Jack Hills:

> Now and again I rebelled in the old way against him, but with an instant sense of treason, when I realised with what silence, as of one possessed of incommunicable knowledge, Vanessa met my plaints. (p. 69)

It is a moment which is suggestive of a link between father and daughter, a troubled sense of connection which I believe Woolf also sought at this stage in order to enable her writing of the memoir.

Analysing the relationship between father and daughter, Virginia Hyman has suggested that what Woolf does in *Reminiscences* is to 'place the three women in the family, her mother, her half sister, and Vanessa, in sequential relationship to her father, while placing herself outside this female constellation, and, by implication, on her father's side'.[46] Not only does Woolf take sides with her father, both Vanessa and Stella are given intimate access to the mother in the memoir which Woolf, as writer, is not. Trying to envisage Vanessa as baby at the beginning of the memoir Woolf imagines the mother's gaze into the baby's face. The effect, partly because of the conventionality of the language and partly because she can only speculate about what the mother sees, is to leave her outside the loving unity of mother and child. This closeness is seen as threatening, even as pathological, when she later describes Stella's relationship with her mother:

> It was beautiful, it was almost excessive; for it had something of the morbid nature of an affection between two people too closely allied for the proper amount of reflection to take place between them; what her mother felt passed almost instantly through Stella's mind; there was no need to ponder and criticise what the soul knew. (p. 50)

What she preceives in this instinctual receptivity of Stella's is the collapsing of identity into undifferentiated merging – the lack of that reflection which, as we have seen in relation to the diary, was a requirement for identity and for the creation of the writer's 'I'. By excluding herself, by not allowing her own intimate relationship with her mother into the memoir but displacing it on to Vanessa and Stella, Woolf maintains her identification with her father and by implication her position as writer. It is important to remember too that she was writing the memoir partly as a response to Vanessa's first pregnancy, an event which must have awakened conflicting feelings. The memoir could also be read as her coming to terms with her displacement by asserting her own different, non-maternal connection with family.

Some thirty years later, in 'A Sketch of the Past', writing again about her early childhood, Woolf was able to discover, through remembering, a way of incorporating her very early relationship with her mother into her writing, 'thinking back through our mothers'.[47] The suggestion to start this sketch is attributed to Vanessa; one of the deeper reasons for its genesis in April 1939 is the Roger Fry biography which Woolf had been writing since 1938 and finding arduous and unpalatable. Sifting through Fry's letters for information to fill the blanks in her knowledge of him, Woolf found herself involved in a kind of detailed and painstaking research to which she was ill-suited. Her diary over the months of writing and revising the biography is full of distress at 'so much fact seeking' and the constraints on her to write a more conventional biography than she had herself, by this time, argued for in her essays:

> I must somehow shorten & loosen; I *cant* (remember) stretch out a long painstaking literal book: later I must generalise & let fly. But then, what about all the letters? How can one cut loose from facts, when there they are, contradicting my theories? A problem. But I'm convinced I cant physically, strain after an RA portrait. (*D*, V, p. 138)

References to her frustration with the Fry work are an important thread within the 'Sketch' itself, suggesting a repressive present from which her memoir then 'cuts loose' into its different past. Woolf finds the freedom of a new position and form – presented as a beyond, a formlessness, within the 'Sketch' – through a negation of the old one and by registering the passage between them. Whilst 'Reminiscences' seems to embody Woolf's desire to incorporate herself into an already established tradition, the 'Sketch' was written literally in the spaces between, in the time that could be liberated from the more conventional ordering of a life in the Fry biography.

Phyllis Rose has suggested a connection between the 'Sketch' and the reading of Freud which Woolf was undertaking at the same time.[48] Whether under Freud's influence or not what Woolf does at the beginning of the 'Sketch' is to try to relinquish conscious control of the structuring of the writing, to allow into it the methods of 'free association' by letting her mind drift towards its own point of stasis or beginning. In an extraordinarily evocative passage, well worth quoting in full, Woolf gives us her 'first memory':

> This was of red and purple flowers on a black ground – my mother's dress; and she was sitting either in a train or in an omnibus, and I was on her lap. I therefore saw the flowers she was wearing very close; and can see purple and red and blue, I think, against the black; they must have been anemones, I suppose. Perhaps we were going to St Ives; more probably, for from the light it must have been evening, we were coming back to London. But it is more convenient artistically to suppose that we were going to St Ives, for that will lead to my other memory, which also seems to be my first memory, and in fact it is the most important of all my memories. If life has a base that it stands upon, if it is a bowl that one fills and fills and fills – then my bowl without doubt stands upon this memory. It is of lying half asleep, half awake, in bed in the nursery at St Ives. It is of hearing the waves breaking, one, two, one, two, behind a yellow blind. It is of hearing the blind draw its little acorn across the floor as the wind blew the blind out. It is of lying and hearing this splash and seeing this light, and feeling, it is almost impossible that I should be here; of feeling the purest ecstasy I can conceive (pp. 74–5).

The moments she recalls are pre-oedipal moments of oneness with her mother's body, the second moment, with its powerful evocation of 'oceanic feelings', symbolically echoing the first. Having excluded her own experience of her mother from 'Reminiscences' Woolf realises it here with delicacy and complexity. The perspective she establishes at the beginning of the quoted passage is foreshortened, collapsing the distance between but within that close-up view of the mother's dress there is also an awareness of foreground and background, the particular colours of the flowers against the void of blackness. This sense of differentiation within an overall unity or continuity is repeated in the rhythm of the waves, pulsations which are also breaks within a continual flow. Marion Milner analysing these very early stages of consciousness has written resonantly of them, using images which echo Woolf's, as 'the dark rhythmic heaving currents and pressures of internal awareness from which the "face" of ego-consciousness recurrently emerges, like a flower out of a dark "earth" or background, or a baby out of a dark womb'.[49] Julia Kristeva has designated this 'rhythmic space' the semiotic chora; she describes it in terms of 'the drives' or 'discrete quantities of energy' moving through the body of the subject who is not yet constituted as such; these are always double, positive and negative, pushing towards the generation of the subject and his/her negation.[50]

The term chora has been 'borrowed' by Kristeva from Plato and means receptacle; she also refers to D.W. Winnicott's idea of 'holding' to explain it. Winnicott believed that the mother holding the child also gives back to the child its own reflection.[51] A sense of an 'inner containing space' – the beginnings of a sense of identity – have therefore in infancy depended on and been experienced through the mother's holding.[52] Milner is again very helpful here in describing this overlapping sense of self and (m)other. She speculates that 'the background awareness of one's own body, that which both holds and is held by, after infancy, must have been largely indistinguishable from the awareness of one's mother's body doing the holding'.[53] Woolf's bowl, which links the two memories is, I believe, her own metaphor for this 'inner containing space': the bowl both supports and receives; it contains but has no boundaries; constituted before the separation of subject and object it can be endlessly filled. Here, as in other places in her writing, Woolf creates a complex sense of space: containing and contained, she encircles the mother who was the original container. The ecstasy she feels, being here, is also experienced within a rhythmic awareness which recalls the mother's body. Again this suggests a simultaneous unity and separateness; remembering she is finding a place where narcissistic pleasure was indissociable from the experience of the (m)other.

Writing these memories Woolf seems to be reaching towards the disappearance of language or the writing subject. She is aware that writing involves her in a process of differentiation – a sorting and naming – which she must impose on the experience in order to give it definition. The recognition of the flowers as anemones, for instance, arises out of a more archaic memory of their colour; similarly the problem of deciding which of the two memories comes first only exists within the ordering of language which demands their placing with reference to a before and after; when they cannot exist – as they obviously do for her – simultaneously.

These 'colour-and-sound' (p. 77) memories as Woolf calls them are spatial memories, essentially unlocated in time. They are associated with a place, St Ives, which exists both as a real place and as a symbolic topography where the memories 'hang together' (p. 77), fuse and join. Woolf suggests how she would paint these first impressions and then later rejects the analogy with a picture because 'sight was always then so mixed with sound' (p. 77). Experienced as within the body as much as outside it, these images have fragile or uncertain borders; sense impressions flow together, move from the more external orientation of seeing to the greater inwardness of hearing:

> I should make a picture that was globular; semi-transparent. I should make a picture of curved petals; of shells; of things that were semi-transparent; I should make curved shapes, showing the light through, but not giving a clear outline. Everything would be large and dim; would come through this petal or leaf – sounds indistinguishable from sights. (p. 76)

If, as Lacan suggests, it is sight which confirms the separation of subject and object, which provides the subject with a unified image of him/herself, contained within boundaries, then Woolf's synaesthesia here with its blurring of divisions, recalls the time before.[54] Memory seems to be gesturing towards the point of its own undoing, creating a space before the subject is constituted within time and within language; the paradox is, of course, that this place only exists retrospectively, nostalgically, when it can be represented.

Woolf's 'moments of being' in 'A Sketch of the Past' could well be interpreted as similarly 'timeless' moments: not specifically connected with her mother's nearness in the way her earliest memories are, they nevertheless could be thought of as 'psychotic' in the sense that Kristeva uses that term: that is they are moments when the subject, returned to the semiotic or pre-oedipal, is lost, shattered by the power of the affect, by cracks opening up in the lining or screen.[55] In her later work Kristeva has used the idea of 'abjection' to mark out the peculiar territory or borderline between the pre-oedipal or semiotic phase and the subject's entry into the symbolic order, the very territory of Woolf's writing. However, the abject, Kristeva believes, is not just a stage within development; it can return, because it is never fully overcome; it goes on threatening the subject with what is never finally repressed or excluded. Elizabeth Grosz comments that the abject is a 'condition' and the 'unpredictable, sporadic *accompaniment*' of symbolic subjectivity:

> It is the underside of a stable subjective identity, an abyss at the borders of the subject's existence, a hole into which the subject may fall when its identity is put into question, for example, in psychosis.[56]

Woolf's 'moments of being' are most often moments when the abyss threatens; but there are other moments, moments of expansion and spaciousness, which again Kristeva, with the link she makes between the abject and the sublime, helps to explain. For Kristeva the abject is experienced as 'a massive and sudden emergence of uncanniness . . . a weight of meaninglessness, about which there is nothing insignificant, and which crushes me'.[57] The sublime, according to Kristeva, is similarly 'objectless'; it carries 'me' through delight and loss somewhere else, somewhere other than where 'I' am: 'The "sublime" object dissolves in the raptures of a bottomless memory . . . It is such a memory which . . . transfers that object to the refulgent point of dazzlement in which I stray in order to be.'[58]

Two of Woolf's 'moments', her fight with Thoby on the lawn (p. 82) and the 'trance of horror' she experiences looking at the appletree and which she associates with Mr Valpy's suicide (pp. 82–3) could well be interpreted as 'massive and sudden emergences of uncanniness' in just the way Kristeva describes. Later she recalls two more: her inability to step across a puddle and the sudden irruption onto her path of an 'idiot boy' (p. 90). The 'dumb horror' of those moments comes back to her later:

> Again I had that hopeless sadness; that collapse I have described before; as if I were passive under some sledge-hammer blow; exposed to a whole avalanche of meaning that had heaped itself up and discharged itself upon me, unprotected, with nothing to ward it off, so that I huddled up at my end of the bath, motionless. (p. 91)

What is significant is that her own sense of disintegration is also a disintegration of her ability to describe the 'object' which has disturbed her. The 'something' which affects her is not 'nothing' but nor is it 'her'; it is somewhere between, drawing her to the edge where subject and object have uncertain borders and where abjection – the sadness she feels here – protects their uncertain separation.

However, there is one 'moment' which she situates between these moments of 'dumb horror' which is different. It is the memory of looking at a flower:

> I was looking at the flower bed by the front door; 'That is the whole', I said. I was looking at a plant with a spread of leaves; and it seemed suddenly plain that the flower itself was a part of the earth; that a ring enclosed what was the flower; and that was the real flower; part earth; part flower. It was a thought I put away as being likely to be very useful later. (p. 82)

This memory partakes of the same imagery as her 'first memory' both in its content and its structure: flower and earth are enclosed in a unity with the earth as the background, or as the 'body' holding the flower. Woolf also implicitly associates this memory with her mother – or with the maternal – through her sense of its 'wholeness'. Later in the memoir this word returns and is applied specifically to her mother. Struggling to find a way of evoking her sense of her mother, Woolf recognises that words cannot get close because her mother is not separate enough to be seen: 'One never got far enough away from her to see her as a person' (p. 96). Her phrase 'the whole thing', (p. 96) becomes a way of describing her and, at the same time, resisting separateness; her mother is absorbed again into 'the whole'.

Woolf's memoir returns to her mother through the experience of loss: this loss of 'wholeness' – and with it the experience of separateness – is, of course, the very condition of remembering. By writing her memoir Woolf attempts to contain the ambivalence of loss by creating a 'benign circle' which will restore her mother to her through her own loving remembrance of her.[59] The sense of her mother as 'central' or as 'whole' is, as we have seen, an attempt to find words for what her mother 'meant' to her, before she had words to explain it. However, by inscribing her mother within the 'circle' of her own writing, Woolf also symbolises her, finding not only words which are the equivalent of her affect, but a form to express it. The idea of writing as a circle whereby she can contain fragmentation within a sense of wholeness again becomes, indeed, the primary 'form' of all her writing for Woolf:

> I make it real by putting it into words. It is only by putting it into words that I make it whole; this wholeness means that it has lost its power to hurt me; it gives me, perhaps because by doing so I take away the pain, a great delight to put the severed parts together. Perhaps this is the strongest pleasure known to me. (p. 84)

Here, her mother – or her mother's loss – is no longer referred to but displaced through the very process of symbol-making which substitutes a form of 'wholeness' for the 'wholeness' of her presence. Woolf, through writing, symbolically replaces her loss, disavows it; she enters into the world of signs and symbols, bringing into existence her 'self' and a wholeness which is separate from her; her joy is the mark of her triumph.

Yet, as we have already seen, this triumph is never securely won for Woolf and she is drawn back again and again to the point of disintegration. No doubt her mother's premature death when Woolf was just 14, intensified and distorted her loss. Woolf records – represents – in the memoir her disturbed, hallucinatory sense of reality at her mother's deathbed which is also, of course, her refusal to *perceive* her mother's death (p. 107). However, it is the experience afterwards, her description of going with George and Nessa to meet Thoby at Paddington,[60] that I want to examine here:

> It was sunset, and the great glass dome at the end of the station was blazing with light. It was glowing yellow and red and the iron girders made a pattern across it. I walked along the platform gazing with rapture at this magnificent blaze of colour, and the train slowly steamed into the station. It impressed and exalted me. It was so vast and fiery red. The contrast of that blaze of light with the shrouded and curtained rooms at Hyde Park Gate was so intense. Also it was that my mother's death unveiled and intensified; made me suddenly develop perceptions, as if a burning glass had been laid over what was shaded and dormant (p. 108).

The contrast of light and darkness could well be seen as evoking again the rhythm of the pre-oedipal waves or that sense of brightness against a darker backgound which was a feature of her earliest memories. As in Kristeva's description of the sublime, light 'dazzles' her, carrying her beyond the particular place or object into the 'bottomless memory' of her mother's death; yet neither is her mother's death the 'object' or focus of the experience, but is rather indistinguishable from the rapturous sense of light. This 'straying' of the subject between memory and perception is expressed in the ambiguity of the phrase, 'it was that my mother's death unveiled and intensified', which hovers between the revelation of the death and the somewhere else, that the death 'unveils', between loss and joy. Woolf's image of the burning glass seems to symbolise the same threat to representation and reflection since the glass is both transparent and opaque, occluding vision through its capturing of light.

Woolf's memoir, as we have noted, is unfinished. Significantly it peters out inconclusively as the young Virginia contemplates the public worlds of men from which she is excluded, which do not 'touch' her:

> There they were, on the verge of the drawing room, these great men: while, round the tea table, George and Gerald and Jack talked of the Post Office, the publishing Office, and the Law Courts. And I, sitting by the table, was quite unable to make any connection. There were so many different worlds: but they were distant from me. I could not make them cohere; nor feel myself in touch with them. (p. 159)

It is as though the point of the memoir has been to recover the bodily closeness which she associates with her mother; at the threshold of this different world – the world of sexual difference – she holds back, seeing it as a foreign country, distant, only concerned with distances.[61]

Sue Roe has suggested that 'A Sketch of the Past' recalls the imagery that recurs throughout Woolf's fiction but that it also provides a 'context' for it, a 'history'.[62] This may be so but I believe the memoir also reveals the process by which Woolf's experiences get dissolved into the problems and processes of writing. The event of her mother's death is represented in the memoir – it is part of the narrative she tells – but it also threatens the whole process of representation, drawing her writing to those difficult edges of horror and delight. It is, of course, important, as Daniel Ferrer has argued, to draw a distinction between the 'madness' of Virginia

Woolf and the madness of language;[63] Woolf's ability to explore those edges is not a further symptom of her own 'disturbed' nature but evidence of her creative ability to follow the difficult journey of subjectivity through the disturbances of language.

It is perhaps appropriate, finally, to return to the image of the burning glass quoted above which Woolf uses in her memoir. It is this image, too, that Luce Irigaray uses in order to think about 'a new despecularization of the maternal and the female'. 'Only when the mirror has concentrated the feeble rays of the eye, of the sun, of the sun-blinded eye, is the secret of the caves illumined', she writes.[64] Like Irigaray, Woolf in her writing is trying to find the 'burning glass' which will allow her to go beyond the limits of representation, to illumine the cave, 'the vast chamber where no-one has yet been'. It is a place which for her, like Irigaray, in spite of the darkness of its non-representation, is: 'Elsewhere. Burning Still'.[65]

CHAPTER FOUR

Vera Brittain: 'Not I but my generation'

In September 1933 Virginia Woolf recorded in her diary that she was reading 'with extreme greed' Vera Brittain's *Testament of Youth*. Yet despite her avid interest in the book – and the approval she candidly awarded it – Woolf cannot resist adding a dash of mockery to her praise, finding its unrelenting account of hardship and deprivation almost too much to take:

> A stringy metallic mind, with I suppose, the sort of taste I should dislike in real life. But her story, told in detail, without reserve, of the war, & how she lost lover & brother, & dabbled her hands in entrails, & was forever seeing the dead, & eating scraps, & sitting five on one WC, runs rapidly, vividly across my eyes. A very good book of its sort. The sort, the hard anguished sort, that the young write; that I could never write. Nor has anyone written that kind of book before. Why now? What urgency is there on them to stand bare in public? She feels that these facts must be made known, in order to help – what? herself partly I suppose. And she has the social conscience. (*D*, IV, p. 177)

Woolf's personal and ideological preference for obliquity, for an approach to the 'truth' which admitted the limits of representation, found itself sorely tested by the 'sort of book' which made a virtue out of documentary realism. This point, of course, could hark back to Woolf's famous indictment of her old opponents, the Edwardian realists, for their inability to deal – as her own art increasingly would – with the 'unknown' and the 'uncircumscribed'.[1] Here, however, she is also responding to a new mood among the young – and a new division in the making – which was driving them, as Woolf saw it, to write nakedly about social issues. The scene is set – and this diary entry exhibits an almost uncanny prescience – for Q.D. Leavis's soon to be launched attack on Woolf for her remoteness from the 'realities of life'.[2] Leavis's criticism was notoriously repeated, though with a new feminist twist, by Elaine Showalter some forty years later when she depicted Woolf as retreating from the political urgencies of a woman's life into sterile aestheticism.[3] A view of the subject as making, or failing to make, political choices bypasses, of course, the question of how the subject is already politically constructed. That the notion of autonomy also needs to be thought about in terms of the political discourses that have produced it as a possibility is an issue that is not irrelevant to this chapter. For the moment, however, I want to stay with the questions that Woolf was pondering in 1933. Why did Vera Brittain write the 'anguished' autobiography that was *Testament of Youth*? Did its writing serve a wider social pupose or did it help the author in some way? And why did she write it now?

Let's start with the last of those questions. 'Now', of course, means not the period of the war itself but between 1929 and 1933 when Vera Brittain was actually writing *Testament of Youth*. In the Foreword to the memoir Brittain suggests, however, that her desire to write about the war and its aftermath had long predated the book she eventually produced:

> For nearly a decade I have wanted, with a growing sense of urgency, to write something which would show what the whole War and post-war period – roughly, from the years leading up to 1914 until about 1925 – has meant to the men and women of my generation, the generation of those boys and girls who grew up just before the War broke out. (p. 11)[4]

Brittain goes on to refer to two previous attempts she had made to write a 'war book'. Her first idea, to write a long novel, foundered on the fact that the events seemed 'too near and too real' to be subjected to 'imaginative, detached reconstruction' (p. 12). Her second idea, to publish part of her wartime diary, was vitiated both by the diary ending too soon to give 'a complete picture' and by the necessary substitution of fictional names which 'made the whole thing seem spurious' (p. 12). *Testament of Youth*, in contradistinction to the distancing and, by implication, falsification of fiction, derives its value, almost self-evidently in Brittain's view, from its 'honest' rendering of experience and endeavour to tell 'the exact truth'.

Yet, for all Brittain makes *Testament of Youth* the culmination of her previous attempts to write about the war, her Foreword does not end with this vindication of her own autobiographical method. Instead she adds a more disturbing reflection on the 'difficulties of perspective' (p. 13) which beset her as she wrote it, seeing these finally as the reason for its 'delay'. Though cast in the form of general reflection, Brittains's sense of unrelatedness to the past still – or perhaps for that very reason – evokes an uncomfortable feeling of dissociation. 'It is almost impossible to see ourselves and our friends and lovers as we really were seven, fifteen or even twenty years ago', she writes, a sentiment which is then resonantly echoed in the passage she quotes from Charles Morgan's *The Fountain*, where past selves become, for the people looking back, 'strange ghosts made in their image, with whom they have no communication' (p. 13). This ghostly otherness haunting Brittain's reflections, takes us back to the problem of distance which Brittain had avowedly turned to autobiography to resolve. Moreover distance is perceived here not only as an estrangement from the events of the past – which it could be argued thus become 'fictional' – but as an otherness within the subject which threatens the very authority and integrity invested in the notion of 'eye-witness'.

One of the crucial discoveries about the effect of traumatic events on the psyche of the sufferer has been that their incidence can be difficult to access or trace, hidden behind the paradoxical symptoms of dissociation or amnesia.[5] Freud, whose insights into trauma stemmed primarily from the neuroses brought on by the experience of the First World War, refers to 'latency' as a way of describing the gap that can occur between the occurrence of a traumatic event and the psychological symptoms it produces.[6] Drawing attention to the significance of this term, Cathy Caruth has perceived an important difference between the repression or unconscious forgetting of an experience and the latency or belatedness of trauma, which means that it is not fully experienced at the time it happens but only 'in connection with another place, and in another time'. As Caruth argues, this has important repercussions for how we conceive of referentiality: 'For history to be a history of trauma means that it is referential precisely to the extent that it is not fully perceived as it occurs.'[7]

It could well be that we should therefore attribute the temporal delay in the writing of *Testament of Youth* – as well as all the other autobiographical memoirs that came out of the war – not wholly to that 'desire to understand what had happened before committing it to paper' that Evelyn Cobley describes[8] but more insidiously to the effects of traumatic memory which could split the experience off from the possibility of its comprehension. This could account, too, for the unintegrated nature of the experience that Brittain describes in her Foreword and perhaps, at least partly, for that persistent theme which runs through writing from the First World War of the difficulties of attempting to translate the experience of war into words. Edmund Blunden, for instance, in his Preliminary to *Undertones of War*, evokes the peculiar 'perplexities of distancing memory' which veils at the same time as it reveals the past; he describes a memory, not yet become a memory, where the sense of immediacy and detail exceed what can be remembered or represented in a narrative of the past.[9] For Siegfried Sassoon, too, back in England after being at the front, the memory of the war presses on his consciousness, refuses to recede into the past but 'insists on being remembered' in a particular and intimate way.[10] As Caruth suggests, the special nature of trauma is that it poses an 'affront to understanding'; integrating the experience into a stable understanding of it therefore risks, in some essential way, its alteration or even loss: 'The capacity to remember', she writes, 'is also the capacity to elide or distort and . . . may mean the capacity simply to forget.'[11]

Given these inhibitions and problems about the representation of wartime experience, it seems significant that the chroniclers of war chose to adopt, as Woolf noted, a documentary approach, which, arguably, limited their ability to challenge the values of continuity and comprehensibility enshrined in the conventions of realism.[12] This must be set in the context, too, of the First World War being seen by many people, both at the time and since, as marking the onset of modernity. To go back for a moment to Virginia Woolf, it would be possible to interpret her writing as, if not directly *about* the war, responding to catastrophic change and the impossibility of representing it. Her novels of the 1920s – *Jacob's Room*, *Mrs Dalloway* and *To the Lighthouse* – all make direct reference to the war, but at a deeper level are also profoundly engaged in finding narrative strategies which break into the security of accepted patterns and suggest the fragility and falsity of 'reality' as we have known it. For Woolf, it was hard to separate her understanding of war from a critique of the dominant masculine ideology. Part of the disturbance of war for her, therefore, was precisely the way it exposed the 'romanticism' or the false idealism at the heart of women's relations, both private and public, with men. In her exploration in *A Room of One's Own* of the way patriarchal values have shaped both history and culture, Woolf makes 1914 a pivotal moment of recognition:

> When the guns fired in August 1914, did the faces of men and women show so plain in each other's eyes that romance was killed? Certainly it was a shock (to women in particular with their illusions about education, and so on) to see the faces of our rulers in the light of the shell-fire. So ugly they looked – German, English, French – so stupid.
> (p. 16)

Woolf, of course, had no direct experience of the war, either in the sense of undertaking war work, or of suffering the impact of its tragedies at first-hand within her own life.[13] For those writers who had been 'there', autobiography, as a discourse which, as Evelyn Cobley suggests, is 'more personal than history but also more authentic than fiction' may have seemed a 'natural' choice.[14] At the same time, however, the immediacy of these autobiographical accounts of the war, and their seemingly 'self-evident' appeal to both writers and readers, should not be allowed to obscure the particular discursive strategies they employ nor, in more general terms, what Regenia Gagnier refers to as 'the pragmatics of self-representation' or 'the purpose an autobiographical statement serves in the life and circumstances of its authors and readers'.[15] This emphasis on context is important when we come to consider how Brittain was responding to and resisting definitions of gender in her writing. For if Woolf, by her adoption of particular narrative strategies, attempts to subvert the dominant structures and traditions in her writing and thus open a space for feminine 'difference', Brittain, by turning to the *same* autobiographical mode as the male chroniclers of war, could also be seen to be engaged in complex negotiations with power and exclusion.

Brittain's Preface to *Testament of Youth* makes no direct reference to questions of gender. However, when Brittain revisited the writing of her war book in her autobiography, *Testament of Experience*, some twenty or so years later, she revealed a strong desire to compete with the previously published masculine accounts of the war. Having noted how 'enthralled' readers were by 'war-books', she goes on to question the assumption that the war 'belonged' solely to men:

> After reading these books, I began to ask: 'Why should these young men have the war to themselves? Didn't women have their war as well? They weren't, as these men make them, only suffering wives and mothers, or callous parasites, or mercenary prostitutes. Does no one remember the women who began their war work with such high ideals, or how grimly they carried on when that flaming faith had crumbled into the grey ashes of disillusion? Who will write the epic of the women who went to war?' (p. 77)[16]

Studying the memoirs of Blunden, Sassoon and Graves with, as she tells us, 'scientific precision', she is convinced that her story 'is as interesting as theirs'; moreover she can offer a different perspective: 'I see things other than they have seen, and some of the things they perceive I see differently' (p. 77). At least partly, therefore, Brittain turns to autobiography, in order to claim the same authority for her – and other women's – story as the men did for theirs. *Testament of Youth* becomes both a record of the past and a way of resisting her own perceived marginalisation in the present.

It is perhaps significant that at the time Brittain wrote *Testament of Youth* she was struggling to make her reputation as a writer. By 1929 she had published two novels, a science fiction work and one non-fictional work, none of which had been particularly successful.[17] As *Testament of Experience* reveals, this was also the period of her life when she was most occupied with being both a wife and a mother and thus torn between her ambitions to write and her domestic responsibilities:

> Sometimes I felt appalled by the load of domestic detail which two small children involved; one understands, I thought after each new avalanche of interruptions, why no woman has ever achieved the concentration demanded by the work of a Shakespeare or a Bernard Shaw. (p. 63)

Finding herself pregnant for the second time just as she begins her 'war-book', she experiences, perhaps inevitably, conflicting feelings:

> Theoretically, I ought to have been delighted; actually, I felt as though I had fallen downstairs. A book involving a large-scale reconstruction of the history, both national and personal, which had shaped my early life could not be tackled effectually with such a major diversion as a new baby ahead. (p. 60)

If this problem of how to put together serious intellectual and creative work with the demands of child-bearing and child-rearing seems an all too familiar one for women, it may well have been intensified by the 'conservatism' of the post-war years and the exaggerated emphasis on women's domestic role which went along with a general hostility to women, particularly married women, taking paid employment.[18] As Deirdre Beddoe points out the number of women in the workforce in this period was lower than in 1911, before the war.[19] Brittain, with her 'semi-detached marriage'[20] and her determination not to abandon her career, was undoubtedly swimming against the popular ideological tide. Yet, as her own disparagement of spinsterhood reveals, Brittain could not detach herself totally from an ideology that promoted marriage as a form of success for a woman, even as she distanced herself from its consequences within her own life and strove for other, more public recognition.[21]

Such contradictions and tensions emerge throughout Brittain's writing. Brittain was an advocate of women's equality and struggled against the assumption of her own insignificance. In *Testament of Experience* she includes an anecdote about 'apologetically' admitting to 'an extremely cultured young male acquaintance named Roy Randall' that she is writing an autobiography. His response, as Brittain records it, is one of disbelief and dismissal: '"An *autobiography!*" he exclaimed incredulously. "But I shouldn't have thought that anything in *your* life was worth recording!"' Brittain then goes on to ponder her own reactions at the time:

> This devastating judgment, though it shook my equilibrium, did not put me off my project. It wasn't Roy's fault that I resembled an immature young woman to whom nothing had ever happened. In spite of my deceptive exterior I did now believe my story to be worth

recording, owing to the very fact – which the cultured Roy had discounted – that it was typical of so many others. (*TE*, p. 79)

The story stands as an indictment of masculine prejudice as well as an indicator of the difficulties faced by a woman who attempts to write autobiographically. At the same time Brittain's response is also revealing. Is she exceptional or typical? Is she unlike the 'immature young woman' she superficially resembles or is the assumption that 'nothing had ever happened' in her life as untrue for other women as it was for her? A similar ambivalence is expressed in Rebecca West's reported defence of her: '"You mean she's not a field-marshal? But it's the psychological sort of autobiography that succeeds nowadays – not the old dull kind"' (*TE*, p. 79). Is it that women, despite appearances, do have stories to tell about the war or must we look elsewhere for 'herstory', reconceptualising autobiography as the story not of public achievement, but of inner, 'psychological' events? Brittain in the end seems unsure how far she wants to claim the same or a different authority for her writing from men. A similar tension could be said to emerge from her *use* of this anecdote. Whilst the story serves to enhance her own public achievement – *Testament of Youth* has, as we already know as we read *Testament of Experience*, led to her triumphant emergence as a best-selling author – she also figures *within* the story as silent and uncertain, letting others speak more openly than she can herself in her own defence.

This deflection of attention away from herself at the very moment when she is attempting to achieve recognition, this doubling of self-assertion with self-abnegation, continually shapes the rhetoric with which Brittain 'justifies' the writing of *Testament of Youth*. In *Testament of Experience*, the drama of her own success as the author of *Testament of Youth* is mitigated by a sense of responsibility towards the 'generation' she represents. As autobiographer, so she at first presents it, she will speak 'not for those in high places, but for my own generation of obscure young women' (*TE*, p. 77). Later, as the book is being written, her own experiences seem subsumed in 'those of all my near contemporaries' (*TE*, p. 80). The book is both for others – an attempt to console those 'who like myself had known despair' – and about others, an elegy for the dead: 'I wrote to commemorate the lives of four young men who because they died too soon would never make books for themselves, yet deserved as much as anyone to be long remembered' (*TE*, p. 80). Her fame, once the book is published, and the long 'struggle in frustrated obscurity' is brought to end, is countered by an injunction to herself 'to keep my head and lay hold on the humility which is most needed when acutely tested'. She goes on:

> Not I, but my generation both living and dead, was the real object of acclaim; how could I avoid the self-importance – one of the least lovable of human qualities – which I had seen overtake other authors on whom fortune had suddenly smiled? (*TE*, p. 97)

How could she, in other words, avoid the association of her achievement with an aggressive 'masculine' drive for success? How could she also situate herself in a 'feminine' discourse of altruism and passivity? Brittain is caught here between avowal and disavowal, relishing her fame and yet, like Woolf before her, fearful of her private and 'lovable' self being overwhelmed by a public, egotistical persona. The notion of her 'generation', the idea that she was writing her autobiography for and about others, seems to offer her a way out, a way of stemming her anxiety, of translating a masculine into a feminine discourse, egotism into altruism. However, the dilemma of difference does not disappear, but returns in the 'different' definitions of her generation that her narrative offers, as both the unrepresented and unrecognised women who contributed to the war and the heroically sacrificed men. Brittain's motives for speaking on behalf of either group are not the same and her altruism, itself a strategy of displacement, is oddly fractured: whilst she can exclude herself and speak for others – seeking an ideal of feminine selflessness and nurturance in relation to men – she must, when writing about her generation of women, include herself and her story, writing against an exclusion which has already happened.

Brittain's problems of how to locate herself as autobiographical subject are not, of course, unique to her, though they are necessarily complicated by how the war and its aftermath affected the meaning of gender. In an influential essay, originally published in 1956, entitled, 'Conditions and Limits of Autobiography', George Gusdorf suggested that any autobiography, however much its author claimed historical disinterestedness for it, was a work of 'personal justification', an attempt on the part of 'the man' who has already lived most of his life to confer meaning on his life by writing about it and thus 'provide a witness that he has not existed in vain'.[22] Yet, as Nancy Miller has pointed out, such self-justification, secretly embarked on in the act of writing autobiography, can only serve to intensify a woman's sense of transgression: in Miller's resonant phrase, for a woman of achievement 'to justify an unorthodox life by writing about it . . . is to *reinscribe* the original violation, to reviolate masculine turf'.[23] 'Personal justification' may thus take on a very different set of meanings for the woman autobiographer: it may signify defence or apology as she attempts to cover her tracks; not self-justification through writing, therefore, but a justification for writing about herself at all.

To take just one brief but almost humorous example of the kind of complicated manoeuvre that a woman may engage in when she enters the masculine field of autobiography: Helena Swanwick was a suffragist and peace campaigner who was described by an associate as 'one of the most commanding personalities of the women's movement'.[24] During the war she had helped to found the Women's International League and after the war was a delegate to the League of Nations. In 1935, four years before her death, she published her autobiography *I Have Been Young*, which Brittain noted in her diary in the same year, expressing a desire to read and review it.[25] In the Preface to her autobiography this eminent campaigner and public figure adopts nonetheless an abject posture: 'To write, nay more, to offer for publication a whole book strung on the thread of one's personality seems an outburst of egotism requiring apology.' This representation of her writing in terms of a loss of self-control recalls a similar moment at the beginning of Alice James's diary. The reasons which Swanwick then goes on to give for her own particular 'outburst' are twofold:

> The first is the wish to express the intense desire which possessed me all my youth for more opportunities for concentration and continuity . . . My other motive was to record, if but briefly and most inadequately, some of the qualities which marked my husband as rare among men.[26]

Whilst her own life becomes exemplary of unsatisfied desire, her husband's 'rare' qualities are seen as a reason for celebration; or to put this another way, Swanwick exalts masculine identity but conceives of her own life only in terms of lack. However, the irony is, as Johanna Alberti has pointed out, that despite 'justifying' her autobiography as in some sense her husband's memorial, after this initial eulogy, Swanwick scarcely mentions him again in the course of the whole book.[27]

In some recent critical accounts of autobiography the idea that women's texts incorporate 'others' into their definitions of self has been seen as an important way of defining their 'difference'. In her ground-breaking essay, 'The Other Voice: Autobiographies of Women Writers', first published in 1980, Mary Mason argued that 'the . . . evolution and delineation of an identity by way of alterity' was a significant and constant element within women's life writing, though this could take various different forms, from the mystical dialogue with a divine other to a generalised sense of communal belonging.[28] Mason interprets this in positive terms – as 'recognition of rather than deference to' the other, even though, at the beginning of the essay she takes a more qualified view, acknowledging how, in the history of the genre, women have had to defend or excuse by this means their transgressive 'excursions' into autobiographical territory.[29] Four years later Susan Friedman extended Mason's arguments into a more assured or positivist theory of difference, maintaining that the model of 'separate and unique selfhood', affirmed and celebrated by Gusdorf, failed to recognise 'the role of collective and relational identities in the individuation process of women and minorities'.[30] Friedman turns to both sociology and psychoanalysis to support her argument, finding in these different sources, that is within women's culturally imposed group identity as well as their development within the family structure, a common trend: that women's self-definition is neither, in her words, 'purely individualistic' nor 'purely collective' but merges 'the shared and the unique'.[31] According to Friedman, therefore, women's auto-biography reflects these developmental patterns, pre-eminently providing women with the opportunity of putting their different sense of self into words.

What is missing from both these accounts, however, is any acknowledgement of that pragmatic or strategic element of autobiographical writing which emerged both in the example of Helena Swanwick's autobiography and in our reading of Brittain's *Testaments*. Commenting on a slightly earlier era, Trev Lynn Broughton has noted wryly that the nineteenth-century ideology of self-sacrifice often masked more complex personal and political manoeuvres by women. 'Feminist history of the Victorian period', she writes, 'fairly bristles with examples of politically deft women appealing to an ethos of self-denial and self-sacrifice in order to justify extraordinary acts of self-promotion, interference and defiance'.[32] To speak of women's identities as relational, as grounded in a concern for others runs the risk of reintroducing the narrative of a stable and continuous self – an ahistorical feminine subject – at the very moment when the universal value and relevance of autonomy is put into question. What at first appear to give importance to context, to the particular relations between self and others, could, at another level, simply be seen as reaffirming a pre-existent and unchanging truth about feminine difference. Paradoxically this notion of a 'different' autobiographical subject could turn out to be not so different but implicated in the same view of the subject as capable of meaning beyond or outside history as the autonomous masculine subject it claims to differentiate itself from; the opposition works to keep both in their place, unchanged and unchanging.[33]

What is so interesting about Brittain's writing, however, are the contradictions, the difficulties she reveals in achieving a consistent subject position. Brittain as autobiographer must seek a place within discourses already marked by sexual difference; the positions she adopts are pragmatic or rhetorical moves within a historical field whose meaning can never be completely known to her. Hence in Brittain's writing a claim to feminine selflessness also reveals and shields an assertion of autonomy whilst the very framing of this binary opposition – the contradictory pairing of autonomy and selflessness – is not a 'natural' or 'timeless' one but itself constructed through and by history. What I want to advance here is an argument about history, about where it is and about how texts or language can provide access to it. It may be that we must begin to see history not in the same terms that Brittain did – as a moment, a crisis, a set of circumstances to be entered upon – but rather as already there within the subject. This is an idea that Naomi Schor suggests in her essay about 'the status of difference' in Georges Sand's writing when she writes: 'history inhabits sexual difference'. According to Schor, trying to understand the meaning of sexual difference, 'peering obsessively into the abyss of sexual difference and its vicissitudes', may mean we miss the crucial way that 'history is already at work in that difference'.[34] While we focus exclusively on the meaning of sexual difference what we may lose sight of, following Schor's argument, are the historical conditions which shaped that particular representation of it; what we may overlook is the problematic way history is neither inside or outside discourse and identity but *both*.[35] The female subject constructed as belonging to the private rather than the political 'masculine' realm and thus seen as occupying a place outside history could *by that very fact* be just as much the subject of a set of historical and political discourses. In many ways, of course, the importance of Brittain to this book is that her autobiographical writing does seem to enter the public world in a different way, to adopt a genre and to assume a much simpler and more confident form of public address than does Alice James's or Virginia Woolf's. War sanctioned a narrative, it seems, that joined Brittain both literally and symbolically to the cataclysmic events of her era, events which decimated and irrevocably transformed her generation. Yet war, so much assumed to belong to the category of the external, the outside, must also be thought about in terms of gender and a particular conception of the subject. Brittain, writing 'for her generation', authorising herself as speaking *for* a momentous historical moment, is also spoken *by* it, by a history which is not where it seems to be, which she is not yet, nor can ever be, wholly in possession of.

The irony of war

In one of the most famous accounts of the literature of the First World War, *The Great War and Modern Memory*, Paul Fussell has claimed that it was only through the development of an ironic vision that the soldier-writers could begin to understand the events they had lived through. Irony, Fussell argued, assisted the processes of memory; it acted as a framing device, a template through which even small and seemingly random events could acquire significance:

> By applying to the past a paradigm of ironic action, a rememberer is enabled to locate, draw forth, and finally shape into significance an event or a moment which otherwise would merge without meaning into the general undifferentiated stream.[36]

However, in Fussell's account irony, with its 'dynamics of hope abridged', also enacts a meaning which is repetitive and inescapable, which 'haunts' the memory, as if this negation of hope or loss of innocence could never finally be understood.[37]

It is this darker view of the meaning and function of irony that Paul de Man, in his essay, 'The Rhetoric of Temporality', allows us to develop. There de Man sees irony in general terms as issuing from 'a relationship within consciousness between two selves'.[38] For de Man irony is 'anything but reassuring': it posits a knowledge of the self as inauthentic; the ironic, 'twofold self' for de Man has undergone a fall, a lapse from innocence which has replaced an 'empirical self', which has existed in a state of mystification, with a linguistic self, which can only endlessly assert the knowledge of its previous inauthenticity. Unlike Fussell, de Man does not see this ironic knowledge as in any way ordering or 'curing' the senselessness of the world; rather it is, at its most extreme, a form of madness, 'a consciousness of non-consciousness, a reflection on madness from the inside of madness itself'.[39] Irony is, according to de Man essentially repetitive, a synchronic structure, which reveals time as neither organic nor continuous:

> Irony divides the flow of temporal experience into a past that is pure mystification and a future that remains harassed forever by a relapse within the inauthentic. It can know this inauthenticity but can never overcome it. It can only restate it and repeat it on an increasingly conscious level.[40]

This account of irony and of how it structures time in terms of irrecoverable distance or difference brings out what is merely implicit in Fussell's account; it challenges the notion – which Fussell as biographer and critic cannot altogether escape from – of a transcendent writing subject who can redeem himself, if not the world, through the order or pattern of writing.

The crisis undergone by the soldiers at the front has often been 'explained', both at the time and since, in terms of how it estranged them from their 'normal' selves; in other words, it is often figured as a form of madness. In his influential study of the First World War, *No Man's Land*, Eric Leed has written that 'the war experience was nothing if not an experience of radical discontinuity on every level of consciousness.' He then goes on to suggest, more generally, how war attacks our very conception of what identity is:

> Continuity often seems to be the sine qua non of identity. An

experience which severs the thick 'tissues of connectivity' that weld separate events into a self is most often viewed as a *loss* of identity. Concepts of identity modeled on the process of maturation and cognitive development often presume something which war effaces: the notion that there is only one self and one sphere of existence.[41]

Put in another way, war could be seen as displacing a belief in the integrity of the subject, a subject who, by definition, is the subject of his or her actions. Paradoxically war is generally represented as the acting out of an intention, the translation of words into deeds; in this way war co-opts a certain definition of the subject. What war in fact demonstrates so emphatically and conclusively is how actions always supersede the subject, flowing towards unthought-of consequences, beyond the subject's control. The irrationality of war is always in fact at odds with the reasons given for it; the subject can no longer constitute himself as governed by reason. War, according to Leed, can be seen as effecting a reversal of 'the normal relationship between actor and action'.[42]

That this crisis of war, a war conducted through the slow attrition of trench warfare and the general mechanisation of fighting which transformed the soldier's role into one of passive waiting rather than heroic action, also needs to be thought of as a crisis of masculinity, a crisis which afflicted men and women differently, has been provocatively argued by Sandra Gilbert in her essay 'Soldier's Heart: Literary Men, Literary Women, and the Great War'. There she sees the war as effecting a brief but dramatic reversal of roles, 'emasculating' the men who had gone to war 'in the hope of becoming heroes', depriving them of their autonomy by 'confining them as closely as any Victorian women had been confined'.[43] Drawing on Leed she goes on to make the connection between the 'hysteria' or shell-shock suffered by soldiers during and after the war with the 'hysteria' previously suffered by women. 'What had been predominantly a disease of women before the war became a disease of men in combat.'[44] It is, of course, in the nature of hysteria, as we have seen, to refuse to stay in its place, and if, as Gilbert argues, men were 'feminized' by the war, this eruption of male hysteria tells us, too, about the 'pathology' of the symbolic order, of what it refuses to know about war or what it cannot successfully incorporate into itself as a form of knowledge. As Jacqueline Rose has argued, war poses a limit to knowledge. At the beginning of the twentieth century the belief that we could ever *know* how to bring war to an end had collapsed. For Freud, therefore, writing in 1932, the question 'why war' was marked, as Rose has demonstrated, by the futility of trying to provide an answer.[45]

Brittain, like the male chroniclers of war, and partly in conscious imitation of them, structured *Testament of Youth* around irony or the 'dynamics of hope abridged', using her wartime diary in ironic counterpoint with a narrative voice which sees beyond her former naivety and hopefulness to its inevitable negation. The diary is quoted and referred to in *Testament of Youth* as a discredited document, a witness to the distance between her past and present selves. 'The naiveties of the diary which I began to write consistently soon after leaving school, and kept up until more than half way through the War, must be read in order to be believed' (p. 43), she writes, anticipating the reader's reaction, and follows this up with a considered, 'mature' view of her diary's significance and its historical 'place':

> The naive quotations from my youthful diary which I have used, and intend to use, are included in this book in order to give some idea of the effect of the War, with its stark disillusionments, its miseries un-mitigated by polite disguise, upon the unsophisticated *ingenue* who 'grew up' (in a purely social sense) just before it broke out. (p. 45)

Brittain looks back to life before the war, a life which for her coincided with her girlhood and adolescence. The picture she draws of pre-war Edwardian England and of provincial middle-class life in that era is one of comfort and complacency. It is an idyll of tranquillity that Brittain lives briefly in terms of her own life and it seems significant that she remembers her relationship with her brother in these early years as being without rancour or difficulty: 'By the time that we both went away to boarding-school he had already become the dearest companion of those brief years of unshadowed adolescence permitted to our condemned generation' (p. 27). Yet her growing up – certainly after the end of her formal schooling – is also marked by her awareness of the gender difference and the conflicts that produces: while her brother is groomed for a career, sent to a public school and then to Oxford, she is expected, not unlike Alice James, to become an 'entirely ornamental young lady' (p. 32), to stay at home, awaiting proposals of marriage and preparing herself for a life of domesticity and motherhood. 'Both for the young women and their mothers, the potential occurrence that loomed largest upon the horizon was marriage', Brittain notes scornfully (p. 33). She, herself, exceptionally, as she believes, entered upon a determined struggle – with little parental or social encouragement – to educate herself and win a scholarship to Oxford. 'Most of the sheltered young women in that era displayed no particular anxiety to have the capacity for thought developed within them' (p. 40), she writes; for Brittain, on the other hand, 'the desire for a more eventful existence and a less restricted horizon had become an obsesssion' and she rejects marriage or the idea of marriage 'as a possible road to freedom' (p. 53).

Testament of Youth is also, of course, a love story: in this case, following a familiar romantic paradigm, it is war which thwarts romance inflicting the almost unendurable pain of separation on the lovers; death brings a tragic yet seemingly inevitable denouement. Roland Leighton, poet and intellectual, the man Brittain falls 'deeply and ardently' in love with (p. 120), is presented as the ideal hero; brooding and slightly mysterious, he seems to fulfil Brittain's longings for a more intense and intellectually satisfying life. Yet Brittains's other narrative, the story she tells about her journey from enclosure to freedom, from parental and social restriction to autonomous activity in the world, provides another structure which is at times at odds with the archetypal patterning of romance and gives Brittain an existence outside it and beyond it. Her hard-won success in gaining entry to Oxford is dismissed by Roland once the war has begun, as an ideal that has become irrelevant, at least for *him*: '"I don't think in the circumstances I could easily bring myself to endure a secluded life of scholastic vegetation. It would seem a somewhat cowardly shirking of my obvious duty"', he writes to her. (p. 103) Brittain is shocked, not surprisingly, given the importance to her of a belief in their intellectual mutuality: '"Scholastic vegetation," hurt just a little; it seemed so definitely to put me outside everything that now counted in life, as well as outside his own interests, and his own career' (p. 104). The threat war poses to Brittain is not just the obvious one of injury or death to the man she loves, but rather another, more insidious separation, brought about by differences of experience. What Brittain fears, so she suggests, is the death of Roland's 'tender' or 'feminine' side:

To this constant anxiety for Roland's life was added, as the end of the fighting moved ever further into an incalculable future, a new fear that the War would come between us – as indeed, with time, the War always did, putting a barrier of indescribable experience between men and the women whom they loved, thrusting horror deeper and deeper inward, linking the dread of spiritual death to the apprehension of physical disaster. Quite early I realised this possibility of a permanent impediment to understanding. 'Sometimes,' I wrote, 'I have feared that even if he gets through, what he has experienced out there may change his ideas and tastes utterly.'

In desperation I began to look carefully through his letters for every vivid word-picture, every characteristic tenderness of phrase which suggested that not merely the body but the spirit that I desired was still in process of survival. (p. 143)

If, on the one hand, war puts in doubt the possibility of equality or even communication between the sexes by removing its basis in 'feminine' sentiment, it could equally be said, as the earlier example showed, to undermine women's striving for 'masculine' knowledge and public achievement, by deeming those goals now unimportant or invalid. The 'barrier of indescribable experience' that Brittain refers to is not just the war, or the war as brutal or brute fact, but the authenticity that the war was felt to impart to the soldiers' experience, whilst depriving those left at home of significance or meaning.

In an important article about the changes in women's role during wartime entitled 'The Double Helix' Margaret and Patrice Higgonet have used that figure to explore the troubling way in which women's 'advances' in terms of social equality and economic independence during the war, were balanced by an equally dramatic 'retreat' in the post-war era. The double helix, for these authors, is a structure in which movement and stability can co-exist; it thus helps to explain, by analogy, the structural impasse of women in society, the way women could remain at the same distance from masculine power and prestige, whatever breakthroughs they made, whatever new positions they took up:

In this social dance, the woman appears to have taken a step forward as the partners change places – but in fact he is still leading her. War alters the vocabulary of feminine dependence . . . and it may even improve the lives of some working women. In the long run, however, the dynamic of gender subordination remains as it was. After the war, the lines of gender can therefore be redrawn to conform to the prewar map of relations between men's and women's roles.[46]

This analysis accords well with Brittain's own sense of disappointment and also suggests the way that war not only effected a separation between the sexes – literally and in many cases fatally removing the men – but also covered over a bleak disparity between the rhetoric of gender equality – espoused by men like Roland – and its political and social effect. Grief drowned out many of the contradictions and death could safely give new life to the ideology of romantic love. Brittain's account of her relationship with Roland is told, of course, in retrospect and derives much of its poignancy from the fact of Roland's death. But death also removed conflict and in the aftermath of his loss Brittain could align her war work as a VAD with his memory as well as her later career at Oxford, without hoping for some 'interested sympathy' from him, the absence of which, before his death, could drive her to fury (p. 217).

So far the contradictions of *Testament of Youth* would seem as if they were both overwhelmed by, and integrated within, the larger narrative of war. However, Brittain also preserved many of those contradictions through her use of irony. 'The ironies of war', Brittain reflects at one point, 'were more than strange; in terms of a rational universe they were quite inexplicable. But now the universe had become irrational and nothing was turning out as it once seemed to have been ordained' (p. 288). For Brittain her 'ironic' use of her diary solved her problems of perspective which had long held up the writing of *Testament of Youth*. She was enabled in this way to signify a 'before and after' structure, the 'division' made in the continuity of her world by war from which, then, all her future life could be dated (p. 317).[47] However, the irrationality she describes seems, by her own account, resistant to linearity, to the ordering of events 'as they have been ordained' and her irony could perhaps better be described as folding the 'before' and 'after' within each other, as arranging them in an overlapping rather than consecutive fashion.

According to de Man, as we have seen, it is precisely the continuity of time that irony puts into question; what it articulates is a radical separation *within* the subject; the subject recognises the past but disavows it as inauthentic; it is not that it once was, but that it both is and has never been. Naomi Schor has posited a connection

between irony and fetishism seeing in both an analogous structure
– not unlike the 'synchronic' structure described by de Man –
whereby something can be simultaneously validated and denied:
'Just as the fetish enables the fetishist simultaneously to recognize
and to deny woman's castration, irony allows the ironist both to
reject and to reappropriate the discourse of reference.'[48] For Vera
Brittain, references to the past such as this one, which involve
quotation from her diary, seem similarly structured; they conjure
up a world which she both ironises and incorporates into her
writing, which she distances herself from, even as she preserves
their memory:

> In those days people's emotions, for all the War's challenge, still
> marched deliberately and circumspectly to their logical conclusion.
>   As I undressed some hours later in the tiny bedroom of my
> grandmother's house, I no longer wondered what I really thought of
> him . . . I hardly waited to throw my woollen dressing-gown over my
> nightdress before seizing the familiar black book and my friendly
> fountain pen.
>   'O Roland,' I wrote, in the religious ecstasy of young love
> sharpened by the War to a poignancy beyond expression, 'Brilliant,
> reserved, extravagant personality – I wonder if I shall have found
> you only to lose you again, or if Time will spare us till it may come
> about that the greatest word in the world – of which now I can only
> think and dare not name – shall be used between us. God knows,
> and will answer.'
>   In spite of the War, the next day was heaven. (pp. 114–15)

   The intensity of the language of the diary entry with its 'sublime'
emotion is immediately deflated by the cliched reference to the
'heavenly' day they in fact spent together. The narrator recognises
the desire expressed by the diary entry but as something excessive
or naive. The diary here – and indeed elsewhere – is used to define
the limits of what can be represented, gesturing 'beyond expression', to a place which, in the structure of the book, becomes a past,
known only in terms of desire or hyperbolic metaphor. The
temporal disjunctions of *Testament of Youth* bring different levels
of language into relation; the present is thus represented as not only
distant from the past but as incompatible with it. Irony is a way of
allowing them to co-exist on different registers. The idealism of the
past is kept at an ironic distance; it becomes a source of interested

and bemused reflection; but more ambiguously, I would suggest, by preserving that idealism, reviving and reincorporating it, the text also uses idealism to invoke – if not to mourn – the limits of realistic representation.

At this point Naomi Schor's essay quoted above, encourages us to go on and ask a further question. What might irony have to do with femininity? How might the oscillations of irony intersect with the writing of sexual difference? It is a question which I want to pursue not through fetishism but through the idea of mourning which could similarly be said to involve a screening process, an ambivalence around the recognition and denial not of an object, in this case, but its loss. In his famous essay, 'Mourning and Melancholia', published in 1917, Freud sought to understand the pathological condition of melancholia through its relation to the normal 'work' of mourning; melancholia, for Freud, involves a similar process of grief but for an object which remains unconscious, which the subject has transposed – internalised – as a loss within itself. Whilst mourning involves a period of confusion and searching for the lost object and a withdrawal from reality, eventually, according to Freud, a 'deference for reality' supervenes and the ego becomes 'free and uninhibited again', able to form fresh libidinal attachments.[49] In melancholia, however, ambivalence – successfully negotiated in mourning – cannot be abandoned without the object also being given up, and the melancholic, turning his hatred against himself, will suffer a 'painful wound'.[50] It is only through the acknowledgement of loss that the work of mourning can be completed; yet the melancholic, we could say, by denying the loss, also lives it endlessly; denies their own existence rather than the loss.

Julia Kristeva has similarly defined mourning in terms of an economy of losses and compensations: both mourning and melancholy for her share 'an intolerance of object loss' and the 'inability to find a valid compensation for the loss'.[51] For Kristeva all losses will ultimately echo or recall the ancient primordial loss, the loss of the mother or the maternal object. Mourning, successfully undertaken, becomes an essential part of the symbolic system, for we learn to speak in the absence of the mother; we accept language as compensation, or as a way of denying her loss by being able to represent it:

Signs are arbitrary because language starts with a *negation* (*Verneinung*) of loss, along with the depression occasioned by mourning. 'I have lost an essential object that happens to be, in the final analysis, my mother,' is what the speaking being seems to be saying. 'But no, I have her again in signs, or rather since I consent to lose her I have not lost her (that is negation), I can recover her in language.'[52]

However, if mourning is a 'normal' aspect of language acquisition, melancholia reflects a crisis in language. For Kristeva, melancholic persons experience a collapse in their ability to signify; they are 'foreigners in their maternal tongue'. They have, according to Kristeva, 'lost the meaning – the value – of their mother tongue for want of losing the mother.'[53] The melancholic for Kristeva, as for Freud, denies their loss, refusing the substitutions of language and thus becomes involved in an 'impossible mourning'. Yet as for Freud, it is the melancholic, who, nostalgically clinging on to the real object – the mother or the mother fantasised as phallic – also suffers 'fundamental sadness', denying not simply the loss but, for Kristeva, the negation of that loss which is the basis of signification.

Vera Brittain, had, of course, reason enough for 'real' grief. In a brief period of three years she lost her fiancé, Roland Leighton, his friends Geoffrey and Victor, and her brother, Edward. *Testament of Youth* is a moving record of the impact of trauma, both the numbing and the 'psychotic' effects of shock, and the slow process of recovery through the work of mourning. At the end of the war Brittain contemplates an 'alien world', a life without all the people with whom she felt intimate. As life begins to resume around her, she finds that she must begin to confront the reality of her losses. 'For the first time I realised, with all that full realisation meant, how completely everything that had hitherto made up my life had vanished with Edward and Roland, with Victor and Geoffrey' (p. 463). Brittain undergoes a prolonged period of searching and disorientation, in much the way Freud describes: she hallucinates her lost objects, or, internalising them, 'entombing' them within her, experiences herself as lost, empty and dead. Only after a pilgrimage to the graves of Roland and Edward in 1921 – an experience which also places their deaths outside herself – does she begin to respond with any hopefulness to life again and to consider herself 'nearly a normal person' (p. 536).

The writing of *Testament of Youth* could also be considered part of the healing process that Brittain underwent, a way of rescuing some meaning from the abyss of war; by putting it into words Brittain could also distance herself from her loss; create both a monument to the dead and a barrier against her own annihilation. The idea to write about Roland forms in Brittain's mind very soon after his death and, although this is put off, she does give in to a 'new' and 'overwhelming' compulsion to write poetry (p. 268). According to Kristeva the 'imaginative experience' is always deeply bound up with sadness and mourning and evidences, in her words, a 'struggle against the symbolic abdication that is germane to depression'.[55] Literary creation becomes both a triumph over loss and the illusion covering the void:

> The imaginative capacity of Western Man . . . is the ability to transfer meaning to the very place where it was lost in death and/or nonmeaning. This is a survival of idealization – the imaginary constitutes a miracle, but it is at the same time its shattering: a self-illusion, nothing but dreams and words, words, words.[56]

This for Kristeva is the 'unease' underlying the symbolic order: that it rests upon 'translation' or a 'ceaseless' transposing of affect into symbol; words ultimately cover an absence; in speaking we are also naming our loss. The artist for Kristeva is often a depressed person in whom memories of loss are revived and who is driven to name the unnameable. Literary creation fills a void; it 'evicts death, protecting the subject from suicide as well as from psychotic attack'.[57] In this sense, writing for Brittain could be, quite literally, her salvation.

However, before Roland's death, there is an interesting moment in the narrative when Brittain recalls herself anticipating the trauma that was to come. In a conversation with Roland before he goes back to the front she tells him – oddly as it seems to him – that she would marry the first reasonable man who asked her if he died because it would allow her all the better to retain his memory:

> 'If one seems to have forgotten, the world lets one alone and thinks one is just like everyone else, but that doesn't matter. One lives one's outer life and they see that, but below it lies memory, unspoiled and intact. By marrying the first reasonable person that asked me, I should thereby be able to keep *you*; my remembrance would live with me always and be my very own.' (p. 186)

Here Brittain seems to be describing precisely the resistance of trauma to representation, its dissociated existence in the realm of indescribable affect: as we have seen the inability to integrate trau-matic experience can also indicate an unwillingness to surrender the memory to change and the normal process of forgetting. Brittain here, it seems, though consciously – and before the trauma which she as writing subject nevertheless recollects – is refusing the compensations of language, unwilling to surrender the 'real thing' (Roland, intimacy with another, originally the mother) to its loss, by translating its absence into words. She will not allow her memory, so she asserts, to enter the world of symbolic exchange, to become part of the same world as the rest of her experience. How far could this imagined act of remembrance by Brittain indicate a resistance to a symbolic order which exacts from us not just the acceptance of loss, but the negation of the loss and the denial or symbolic killing of the (m)other?

Testament of Youth was in fact written after Brittain's marriage, a marriage which to begin with involved her in much heart-searching about what she owed to her husband and whether she could also, nevertheless, keep faith with Roland. Brittain's decision, unlike her earlier fantasised one, is that she must 'dissociate' herself from her past in order to ensure a future (p. 651). However, Brittain's dilemma in marrying was also, as she saw it, that it constituted her as a 'married woman', safely defined in terms of the patriarchal order, enclosed with its interior domestic space:

> Marriage . . . could never, I now knew, mean a 'living happily ever after'; on the contrary it would involve another protracted struggle, a new fight against the tradition which identified wifehood with the imprisoning limitations of a kitchen and four walls, against the prejudices and regulations which still made success in any field more difficult for the married woman than for the spinster. (p. 654)

As we have seen, *Testament of Youth*, became the vehicle by which Brittain created for herself the identity of author, and constituted a life for herself beyond marriage. However, at this point, it seems significant, too, that she did so by means of a work which returned her to the scene of her earlier losses and which invoked a mourning – a melancholia – which had never been overcome. *Testament of Youth* both tells the story of a willed and courageous act of survival, of mourning successfully undertaken which leads her back slowly to 'normality' and the 'melancholic' survival of an 'imaginary' past, which makes both language and temporality strange. Kristeva believed that for the melancholic 'an overinflated, hyperbolic past fills all the dimensions of psychic continuity'.[58] This seems an apt description of that 'other' language that Brittain ironises in *Testament of Youth*, and which also represents an 'otherness' in terms of her self which cannot be assimilated into the order of events, a difference which resists its disappearance in the order of the same. As Brittain noted bitterly, after the war, the 'excessive population' of women who had 'inconsiderately failed to die in large numbers' during the war was often described as 'superfluous' (p. 577). It may not be too much to suggest that there exists a correlation between this embarrassing, superfluity or surplus of women, disempowered and discredited by the patriarchal order, and the 'excess' which disturbs Brittain's memoir, an alterity which she returns to, and which remains outside realism, a voice of desire and lamentation – as is the voice that speaks to us in the diary – drawn to limits and edges.

And history? When Brittain went back to Oxford after the war, she decided to change her course of study from English to History. She explains this in terms of her desire to understand the war: 'After the first dismayed sense of isolation in an alien peace-time world, such rationality as I still possessed reasserted itself in a desire to understand how the whole calamity had happened' (p. 471). Brittain's need to comprehend the past leads her to value reason and rationality and to conceive of the future in terms of imperatives and obligations. Brittain makes a 'rational' decision to marry and we could see the writing of *Testament of Youth* too in terms of its 'realism', its claim to referential 'truth' and the construction of a subject who 'knows'. Yet, this text also provides a way of reading history through a hiatus or a delay, through what the subject cannot integrate in terms of knowledge but ironically displaces or disavows. This chapter, like the next, asks the question of how the female subject can be written into a symbolic which violently casts out alterity as madness or death. In an irony that finally escaped her, Brittain, in mourning the men that were killed, also registers and reflects the strangeness of her own act of self-representation.

CHAPTER FIVE

Sylvia Plath: ' "I" and "you" and "Sylvia" '[1]

The front cover of *The Journals of Sylvia Plath*, the edited compilation of Plath's journals that was published in 1982,[2] almost twenty years after her death, prominently displays the claim by its publishers that the book is: *In her own words, the true story behind The Bell Jar*. This assertion is repeated and amplified on the back cover:

> No other major contemporary American writer has inspired such intense curiosity about her life as Sylvia Plath. Now, the intimate and eloquent personal diaries of the twentieth century's most important female poet reveal for the first time the true story behind *The Bell Jar* and her tragic suicide at thirty.

A discussion of Plath's relation to autobiography can hardly fail to take note of the fact that Plath's life has provided the most common or advertised route into her work. Reading autobiographically, we have been told, is the only way we *can* read her writing. Her novel, *The Bell Jar*, has frequently been described as if it offered only the thinnest of fictional disguises to the 'true story' of her life.[3] In the above quotation *The Journals* are promoted by its publishers as if they pulled away the final veil, laying bare Plath's most intimate and private self. Referring to the way the 'mystery' of Plath's death stirred up questions about the boundary between life and art the critic and biographer Linda Wagner has commented:

> For a young woman to kill herself at the beginning of a successful

writing career posed an intriguing – and frightening – mystery. All kinds of equations between art and life began to be suggested . . . Controversy was rampant, and criticism of Plath's work would never again be untouched by biography.[4]

Rampant seems just the right word for some of the more excited and unsavoury critical responses to Plath and it is difficult not to begin to hear a perverse echo of the hysteria so often attributed to Plath sounding, with greater or lesser intensity, in the language of her critics.[5]

This is, of course, the point made to such good effect in Jacqueline Rose's ground-breaking book *The Haunting of Sylvia Plath*. In a chapter in which she examines the excesses of Plath criticism, Rose has seen some of the more grossly sexualized language of writing about Plath as a form of projection, the casting out by Plath's critics of what is most troubling about her writing, only for it to return all the more luridly as image within their own critical texts. Plath's writing, according to Rose, puts various boundaries into question – sexual, psychic, cultural – which then must be all the more forcefully redrawn by the expulsion of Plath's texts to a place beyond, by the denial of the reader's own implication in them. In this view femininity is both 'the fact . . . that appals' with its threat of otherness and a figure to which various different threats and dangers can be related.[6] The question of what Plath's critics are writing about when they write about her is an appropriate one: to adopt Neil Hertz's terminology Plath becomes – and as Rose demonstrates – a kind of 'medusa fantasy', a substitute symbol for what terrifies; which, by the very process of becoming a symbol, structures and therefore simplifies the anxiety.[7] The result is, paradoxically, a freezing of the meaning of Plath's writing, the changing of historical and literary complexity into an icon. For Rose, Plath becomes 'the horror of which she speaks'[8] and we can see the way in which, trapped within a vacuum, or to use Plath's own image a 'bell jar', she can be read by her critics – and perhaps needs to be – as writing always and only about herself.

What does this mean for my own reading of Plath's autobiographical writings, especially for her novel, *The Bell Jar*, if the focus on the autobiographical in Plath's work turns out to be the result of a critical fixation, a way of disregarding what is most unsettling about her writing? Part of the point of including Plath in this book is, I would argue, not to repeat the closed circle which makes Plath and her problems – or the critic's own version of them – stand in for the problems of her texts but to attempt to explore the problematic of her writing itself, particularly the way it can be seen to refuse a settled identity, moving restlesly between different versions of her 'self' and different cultural forms. But behind that there is a more general question which makes Plath an important and intriguing subject for this book: more than most Plath's writing exposes how deeply genre is intertwined with gender. For the issue needing to be raised in Plath's case may be less how do we classify her novel – is it fact or fiction – than what is at stake for her critics when they read it autobiographically? What is at stake for Plath herself in writing fiction? And how has the conventionally hystericised figure of Plath helped to sort out the boundaries of genre as well as stabilise the meaning of gender?

Turning to Plath's writing, indeed one of her earliest surviving atttempts to write about herself, what we find, appropriately enough, is the issue of control – how far is she in control of her own life, her own writing – being raised by Plath in general, existential terms long before it is played back to us as *her* problem by her critics. In 1950, the year she entered Smith College, Plath wrote in her journal:

> Cats have nine lives, the saying goes. You have one; and somewhere along the thin, tenuous thread of your existence there is the black knot, the stopped heartbeat that spells the end of this particular individual which is spelled 'I' and 'you' and 'Sylvia'. So you wonder how to act, and how to be – and you wonder about values and attitudes. In the relativism and despair, in the waiting for the bombs to begin, for the blood (now spurting in Korea, in Germany, in Russia) to flow and trickle before your own eyes, you wonder with a quick sick fear how to cling to earth, to the seeds of grass and life. You wonder about your eighteen years, ricocheting between a stubborn determination that you've done well . . . and a fear that you *haven't* done well enough. (pp. 24–5)

Plath, it seems, is here is suspended between two meanings of the word 'spell' which she uses in quick succession in the same sentence, almost as if the first usage had summoned up the second. When she first uses the word – 'spells the end' – she is referring to how her destiny is already determined, spelt out, by the materiality of existence, by the inevitable fact of death; the second time she uses the word – 'spelled "I" and "you" and "Sylvia"' – she is referring to the way language offers a variety of positions or pronouns – spellings – through which to represent her 'self'; the apparent poignancy of the reflection is that this linguistic plurality is nevertheless contained by the singleness of her fate, the fact she has only one life. Yet we could also read another message into what Plath is saying here. Language is 'open', in the way Plath suggests, to various pronouns as well as syntactic structures through which our relation to it is mediated; however, it is this very openness which itself proves that 'I' am never the unified self of my imagination, with supreme power to order meaning but rather subject to the fleeting stability of the sign. Acutely aware of dualism, of the splitting between mind and body, Plath's anguish is not only that mortality places a limit on our capacity to make meaning, but that language is never adequate to the body, that it spins away from us into equivocation and uncertainty. Language, in this sense, both controls us, has already usurped our power to signify, and is out of control, provoking and calling up meanings of its own. Plath's 'ricocheting' between mutually exclusive estimates of her own worth, feeling at the same time both baffled and oppressed – a theme we can find in many different forms in her writing – has much to do with this sense of a subject at once set free, or set adrift, into the uncertainty of meaning yet already given meaning by her culture and the signs it employs.[9] Hence we can also understand her return to the body in this passage, not as a carrier of death now, but as a possible ideal or idealised source of connection with the world, a place of fertility or creativity beyond words: 'how to cling to the earth, to the seeds of grass and life'.

What is also noteworthy about this passage is that Plath places herself and her reflections with reference to politics and history. If the 'myth' of Plath is that she used history as a source of imagery for her own psychic pain, absorbing the external into her internal world, here, at least, she seems to be expressing a more complex dynamic between the social and the psychic. Responding to the events of 1950, which included the making public of America's decision to construct the hydrogen bomb, as well as the intensification of military action in Korea, by imagining violence becoming real or visible, invading her consciousness (after it already has), could both be described as paranoid at the same time as it takes us

far beyond any description of the individual psyche. Indeed the
question of where to attribute the threat – is it inside or outside –
could be seen as the key question of Plath's era and culture,
producing the need for ever more stringent policing of the
boundary. According to Andrew Ross: 'Cold war culture . . . was
crucially organised around the interplay between what was
foreign, and outside, and what was domestic, and inside.'[10] The
most extreme illustration of this policing, of a need to identify and
eject 'the enemy within' came with the arrest in the summer of
1950 – the same year as Plath's journal entry – of Ethel and Julius
Rosenberg and their trial as traitors for having allegedly handed
over the secret of the atomic bomb to the Russians; their execution
in June 1953 is, of course, referred to by Plath in her ominously
flat-toned opening to *The Bell Jar*: 'It was a queer, sultry summer,
the summer they electrocuted the Rosenbergs, and I didn't know
what I was doing in New York.'[11] What the Rosenbergs came to
illustrate, according to Ross (and what Plath's prose appears to
pick up) was how ordinary lives could conceal or mask what was
foreign and threatening; paradoxically, therefore, 'every further
revelation about the humdrum petty-bourgeois reality of their
lives served not to dull but to heighten the already "monstrous"
status of the Rosenbergs' alleged crime'.[12] Plath, anxiously
surveying her own life and psyche for flaws, trying to separate
what is authentic from what is a 'cover-up',[13] could as much be
seen as speaking for her culture as for herself. What is so difficult
is that Plath must attempt to locate herself – even when she is at
her most critical of her society – in terms of the very divisions
which cold war culture used to exert its strongest control over the
individual.

Nothing does more to illustrate or reinforce this point than
Plath's complex negotiations with questions of gender. To begin
with Plath, aged 18, registered in her journal her resistance to a
femininity she saw as positioning her as secondary or Other. 'I am
at odds. I dislike being a girl, because as such I must come to realize
that I cannot be a man. In other words, I must pour my energies
through the direction and force of my mate' (p. 23). Seven years
later, what she had called, in self-castigating tones – which
possibility owed something to the popular Freudianism of her day[14]
– her 'envy' of the man, 'born of the desire to be active and doing,
not passive and listening' (pp. 34–5) had been sublimated into the

idea of a man 'big enough' to make the sacrifice worthwhile. Her husband Ted Hughes became, for Plath, her 'saviour':

> This is the man the unsatisfied ladies scan the stories of *The Ladies' Home Journal* for, the man women read romantic women's novels for: oh, he is unbelievable and the more so because he is my husband and I love cooking for him (made a lemon layer cake last night) and being secretary, and all. (p. 220)

That Plath should return later in her life to her fear of passivity – or that her devotion to Hughes should turn out to be another version of the passivity she feared – is not perhaps surprising. By 1959 she was writing in her journal: 'I have no life separate from his, am likely to become a mere accessory . . . I am inclined to go passive, and let Ted be my social self' (p. 326). What is more difficult to understand is Plath's relation to 'mass-produced fantasy'[15] as well as the way such fantasies position female desire. In 1962, separated from Hughes, she made *The Ladies Home Journal*, which, according to Barbara Ehrenreich and Deirdre English had been the 'propagandist of domestic felicity for three generations of women' her scornful target;[16] in a famous, often quoted passage in a letter to her mother, she bitterly elides 'motherly' advice with the popular magazine she now purports to despise:

> Don't talk to me about the world needing cheerful stuff! . . . It is much more help for me, for example, to know that people are divorced and go through hell, than to hear about happy marriages. Let the *Ladies' Home Journal* blither about those.[17]

But how do we equate this with the Plath who had once unashamedly linked herself with the *Ladies Home Journal*, allowing it to fashion her desires as a woman but also, perhaps even more remarkably, as a writer of stories? 'I shall have fulfilled a very long-time ambition if a story of mine ever makes the *LHJ*',[18] she wrote to her mother just a year before the letter quoted above, confirming at the same time just how important and well-established that aspiration was.[19]

One explanation may be found in the work undertaken recently by feminist critics on 'women's genres' and in particular on popular romance: what these critics have suggested is that it would be wrong to categorise this genre too simply as constructing 'coercive and stereotyping narratives',[20] which lull their readers into a state of false consciousness. Conceiving of the way romance can have 'complex political effects'[21] – supporting active needs despite seemingly representing passive roles for women – challenges the idea that the place it occupies within culture is either static or single. Tania Modleski, for instance, has seen the distance and superiority of the reading process itself as important, overlaying, to some extent, the reader's close emotional involvement with the heroine:

> Since the reader knows the formula, she is superior in wisdom to the heroine and thus detached from her. The reader, then, achieves a very close emotional identification with the heroine partly because she is intellectually *distanced* from her and does not have to suffer the heroine's confusion.[22]

Paradoxically romance can thus offer the individual reader the possibility of enjoying power: power in relation to the text whose secret, as Modleski suggests, the reader already knows; but power may also be the appeal of the fantasy played out in the text for within the world of romance (and only within the world of romance?) female sexuality can finally overpower the seemingly omnipotent male; the patriarch's power can become 'harnessed', as Rosalind Coward puts it, to one '"special" woman'.[23]

Turning back to Plath's journal entry which contains her description of Hughes as 'the man women read romantic novels for', it is possible to see Plath's remarks as fitting this analysis quite well. Plath also engages in a complex interaction with the idea of popular romance, using it as a paradigm for 'life' at the same time as achieving detachment from it as a 'fiction'. Like other readers of romance, she seeks ways of being unlike the others, of establishing her own unique power and superiority. In Plath's case, the difference between her and the 'unsatisfied ladies' who read romances lies not in the nature of the desires themselves, the compelling fantasy, but in the fact that, like the heroine of the novel, she alone can claim possession of the man. According to Plath Hughes 'unbelievably' fulfils the stereotype of popular romance – he is real – at the same time that he thus saves her, or so she believes, from a 'feminine' preoccupation with fantasy. Ironically, however, we could argue, that Plath is thus empowered in the very terms set out by romance – through her union with *his* power – and can distance herself from popular romance and its readers only by a form of wish-fulfilment which transforms life itself into a novel.

The point may be as we have seen – and as Plath here seems to demonstrate – that popular romance provides an ambiguous place of identification, a site of conflicting desires for power as well as romantic fulfilment, desires that can be resisted as well as embraced; but it can as easily – and Plath is again a case in point – fold the subject back into a world already shaped by the conventions of romance. The difficulty, therefore, may be less how we locate the woman within the system of meanings offered by romance – how we account for the complex and perhaps even contradictory relation of the reader to the text – than how we locate her with any certainty outside, how we ever arrive at a place completely exterior to it. As Tania Modelski has argued the conventions of romance are 'part of our cultural heritage as women',[24] inescapably part of the ideology we exist within: 'We are all victims, down to the very depths of our psyches, of political and cultural domination (even though we are never only victims).'[25]

This proves important in a more general sense when we are considering Plath in 1957 about to embark on the novel that was eventually to become *The Bell Jar*.and anxiously contemplating the kind of novel she wanted to write. To begin with she runs through a number of possible models, all men:

> I could write a terrific novel. The tone is the problem. I'd like it to be serious, tragic, yet gay & rich & creative. I need a master, several masters. Lawrence, except in *Women in Love*, is too bare, too journalistic in his style. Henry James too elaborate, too calm & well-mannered. Joyce Cary I like. I have that fresh, brazen colloquial voice. Or J.D. Salinger. But that needs an 'I' speaker, which is so limiting. Or Jack Burden. I have time. I must tell myself I have time.
> (p. 156)

What this slightly motley list suggests is Plath's difficulty in settling on not just a voice but beyond that, her cultural place, her potential readership. The idea of her as literary apprentice learning from a 'master' is also somewhat diluted by her adoption of 'several masters' and the impression she gives of weighing up their attractions against each other. Moreover in the next breath, or the next paragraph, Plath can contemplate slipping out from under the oppressive 'weight' of 'all the witty, clever, serious prolific ones' altogether and 'selling her soul' by writing a best seller:

> I feel, were it not for Ted, I'd sell my soul. It is so ironic to think of nobly writing and writing on this novel, and sacrificing friends & leisure & turning out a bad bad novel. But I feel I could write a best seller. (p. 156)

Plath's language accurately reflects the heroic and implicitly masculine endeavour of high literary culture which she can imaginatively free herself from – and find greater belief and confidence in her own powers – through the imaginative licence of the 'best seller'. The time which Plath earlier tried to reassure herself that she had (and feared that she had not) is here construed in terms of a masculine economy of achievement and sacrifice: to become a creator of high culture means to subordinate time and pleasure to 'art'; the 'best seller' is on the side of leisure: an idea of time which escapes the masculine economy by the very fact of its being undirected or aimless.

Plath's uneasiness about positioning herself as a novelist must at least in part have to do with this gendering of a division which sets authentic literary activity over against the consumer-oriented mass market. Implicitly Plath could envisage writing a great novel only as a form of masculine mimicry, by subordinating herself to a 'master'; but the thought of the 'best-seller' which seems briefly to energise her, in another way also poses a threat to her autonomy as a writer. For if popular genres have become in the history of literary culture the feminised other of an imagined artistic autonomy – if the production of meaning within popular genres and *only* there is seen as passive and conventional – then Plath, writing in the first person about love and sexuality, faces the problem of how to differentiate her work from the popular form of 'true confession' it seems to resemble; how to secure *her* autonomy against its displacement and absorption into this generic form. The same entry in her journal sees her turning away from the idea of the best seller to reaffirm that her novel can be 'in its small way' an 'artwork':

> About the voyage of a girl through destruction, hatred and despair to seek and to find the meaning of the redemptive power of love . . . Well-written sex could be noble & gut-shaking. Badly, it is true confession. And no amount of introspection can cure it. (p. 157)

Not only can introspection not provide a cure, it can only, we might argue, exacerbate the problem, confirming her further in her ideological place. The act of turning inwards cannot alleviate the inevitable splitting involved in self-representation, the displacement of a desired private core of selfhood on to the forms of public expression. So, as Plath partly perceives, the very attempt to take control of the meaning of her experience through introspection runs the risk of becoming merely the passive illustration of an already established convention, self-defeating in the most literal sense, binding female subjectivity ever more intimately to a form of cultural and ideological constraint.[26]

Eventually, however, Plath did, of course, settle on first-person narration for her novel despite the risks and despite her fear about its 'limiting' effect on her writing. Nevertheless her journal also reveals her trying to retain authority over the meaning of her text – to be its author in the sense accorded that term by high culture – by opening up a gap between the 'I' of the novel and her own point of view:

> Then: the magazine story: written seriously but easily, because it is easier to manipulate strictly limited characters, almost caricatures, some of them, than the diary 'I' of the novel, who must also become, in her way limited, but only so that she can grow to the vision I have now of life, which tomorrow will be a fuller vision, and tomorrow. (p. 164)

The construction is awkward, even nonsensical: the 'I' of the novel must 'become' limited by being deprived of a knowledge she presumably already has. However, relating this passage from the journal to the previous ones we have looked at, it could be argued that Plath is here attempting to ward off the relegation of the female subject to one side of a cultural divide by also taking up a position of knowledge – the 'fuller vision' her protagonist will grow into – on the other. The disparity between the narrator and the protagonist, or between an older and younger 'I' – the sense of limitation that would allow her to 'manipulate' the character just as she could the characters in the 'magazine story' – thus partly functions as a way of creating some opposition or resistance to the ideology of gender. Perhaps surprisingly – but for us significantly as well – within the network of meanings around popular and high culture, genre and femininity, the autobiographical or confessional mode could be thought of by Plath, despite its apparent 'realism', as subsuming her originality. It is this threat we could interpret her as attempting to combat through a deliberate process of framing and distancing in her novel, creating a space in which she could explore definitions of the female subject both in, and we could add, *as* fiction.

But at the same time a difficulty recurs. Plath could move *across* cultural forms, finding identification with either side of the 'serious' or 'popular' divide to some degree unsatisfactory or uncomfortable, but what she also she reveals in her journal – both consciously and unconsciously – is the persistency with which this opposition reinstates itself in some form or another, enforcing in the process the subordination of the inferior or 'feminine' term. In her journal Plath sometimes figured her relation to writing in blatantly sexual and sometimes disturbingly violent terms. For instance in an entry for 1950, as she early on gives voice to her literary ambition, she conjures a scene which is both private – gratifying in ways that she fears will not be understood – and painful. 'How can I tell Bob that my happiness streams from having wrenched a piece out of my life, a piece of hurt and beauty, and transformed it to typewritten words on paper' (p. 16). Here Plath shifts positions between active and passive, the subject doing and the life being done to but the opposition – writing forcefully acting on a passive body of material – remains the same. This imagery is picked up later in her journal where she talks about 'the virginal page, white' and 'the painful, botched rape of the first page' (p. 162). Almost immediately, however, she follows this with a description of the 'travail' of creativity in terms which are unmistakably 'feminine':

> Slowly, with great hurt, like giving birth to some endless and primeval baby, I lie and let the sensations spring up, look at themselves and record themselves in words: the blind moves in and out on the window with a slight breeze, pale yellow-brown, tawn, and the curtains move, cotton with yellow sun-burst flowers and black twigs on a white ground. (p. 162)

Curiously, the detail of the blind, the sense of colour and movement and the awareness of foreground and background, all recall Virginia Woolf's evocation of her own origins within the pre-oedipal or semiotic in 'A Sketch of the Past'.[27] However, if this passage seems to offer an alternative, gentler, 'feminine' account of creativity to put alongside the previously discussed images of force, the associations of the woman's body with passivity and pain mean that it can also easily be contained within the traditional oppositions of masculine and feminine. Meditating on relationships in her journal in 1952 Plath considered that 'it is not a black and white choice'. 'Sure', she wrote, 'I'm a little scared of being dominated . . . But that doesn't mean I, ipso facto, want to *dominate*' (p. 43). But the scenario of 'devouring and subordination' (p. 42) was also difficult for her to avoid as a way of structuring her own understanding of pleasure and power and the opposition she wanted to resist – the drives as destructive of either self or other – metaphorically at least, kept returning.

Why should writing involve images of violence? And what is the relationship between 'metaphorical' violence and the specificity of its social forms? Where and how do the metaphors relate to the body or to how we live as embodied subjects in social and gendered terms? These questions, crucial to feminism, have not been fully addressed in an approach which would see this violence as an 'effect' of writing, as the inevitable consequence or cost of representation. In his famous and influential post-structuralist essay on autobiography, 'Autobiography as De-facement', which I shall consider only very briefly here, Paul de Man argues first of all that autobiography is less a genre in its own right than a 'figure of reading'; he then goes on to describe a paradox in relation to autobiography: for those very moments which we as readers recognise as autobiographical, the 'specular moments' when an author becomes the subject of his own understanding, depend, according to de Man, on a linguistic structure, on a trope or rhetorical figure. Representing the self, therefore, also threatens the self with its obliteration by language. Taking his examples from Wordsworth's autobiographical writings de Man interprets various images of dis-figurement within Wordsworth's texts allegorically, as figuring the effects of language itself, the way in which the substitutions of language simultaneously give a face and take it away, create faces thus veiling their own de-facement.[28]

De Man makes no explicit reference to gender yet, as other critics have pointed out, the workings of sexual difference are neither absent from the theories he constructs nor the texts which attracted him.[29] For if, as de Man argues, language inflicts a violence on the subject, that violence can then in part be deflected or excised by giving the victim a woman's face; the subject can be rescued from anxiety by making the figure, or the disturbingly figurative aspects of language, feminine. 'When these dramas turn violent', Neil Hertz has commented, 'women are frequently the victims of choice'.[30] De Man's idea of the revolving door which he uses to express the impossibility of trying to hold open a distinction between autobiography and fiction could well be given another turn here: for if sexual difference seems to mask, if not resolve, a violence which has to do with writing itself, we could equally argue that this 'violence of rhetoric' is inseparable from notions of gender and and cannot be thought outside it; that it becomes, in effect, a 'rhetoric of violence'.[31] This is not to suggest that gender precedes discourse or that it does not itself involve problems of representation. But at the same time it may be possible to argue, as Teresa de Lauretis does, that there is 'a weight' within the notion of sexual difference coming from our lived relations, from 'experience' or 'habit', a 'conservative force' working against attempts to rethink it, attempts such as we have seen Plath make when she moves across cultural forms.[32] If, then, according to this argument, gender adds another unsettling twist to the relationship between the fictive or the figurative and the real, the violence written into the oppositions of discourse poses, at the most extreme, the problematic relationship of the subject – any subject – to its culturally positioned object, to the female or feminine body.[33]

Myself, only in disguise

The Bell Jar was published in England in January 1963, a month before Plath's death, under the pseudonym Victoria Lucas; it was reissued in 1966 under Plath's own name, though the secret of its author's identity had become known long before. Publication in the States was delayed until 1971 and when it was finally published there the text of the novel carried with it, almost as a warning, a biographical note quoting Aurelia Plath's objections to the novel being published at all:

> Practically every character in The Bell Jar represents someone – often a caricature – who Sylvia loved; each person had given freely

of time, thought, affection, and in one case, financial help during those agonizing six months of breakdown in 1953 . . . as this book stands by itself it represents the basest ingratitude. That was not the basis of Sylvia's personality . . . [34]

The mother's need to defend her daughter against Plath the author (and by doing so, of course, also defend herself) painfully reveals her private feelings. Presumably the background for this comment (and its publication) was the trend, quickly established after Plath's death, of reading the novel as if it were simply 'true'; paradoxically, however, Aurelia Plath only adds to the sense of disclosure since her claim of falsification also concedes a factual basis to the novel, seems to verify its reference, however distorted, to real people. Plath's pseudonymous authorship of the novel could be seen in a similar light, invested with the same ambivalence: for if it is interpreted, as it commonly has been, as an attempt to protect her family and friends, this disguising of her identity could prove all the more conclusively that the novel really *is* about her, her life; that she is trying to conceal behind a different name the dangerously exposing nature of the text itself.

However, this language of concealment and exposure does not seem altogether appropriate, simplifying, as it does, the problem of referentiality by suggesting that there is some truth, some irreducible fact, that we can discover *behind* the text itself. In what sense, we may ask, does a novel stop being a fiction because it has some relation to real life? And in the realm of fiction what counts as truth – what are we talking about – the truth of fantasy or the truth of fact?[35] It is interesting to relate these questions to Philippe Lejeune's famous attempt to found a theory of autobiography on the factual 'evidence' of the authorial signature, for ultimately this theory too could be said to founder on the impossibility of translating the 'tropological' language of literature – a language inevitably caught in de Man's revolving door – into statements that can be proved either true or false. Lejeune's original proposition about autobiography, it is fair to say, is more complex than those I have been outlining: autobiography, for Lejeune, is to be defined primarily not so much through what a text is – its status as a form of representation – as how it gets read, an assumption that the reader brings to a text in the light of an 'autobiographical contract' set up between author and reader. Yet the kind of reading Lejeune envisages also ends up policing or judging the text for its authenticity, unwilling, so it seems, to take account of a different, more uneasy relation on the part of the reader to the text's literary or figurative nature.[36] Nor can it comprehend the way reading may be historically variable, subject to factors which lie outside any jurisdiction.[37] What difference, for instance, does gender make? Indeed it is interesting to ask how far gender disturbs the whole juridical framework within which Lejeune places autobiography, for if woman's status under the law is not and has not been equal, is her signature necessarily valid or binding in the same way?

It is partly in response to Lejeune that Nancy Miller has set out her case for a '*double* reading' of women's texts, a reading which would 'privilege neither the autobiography nor the fiction, but take the two writings together in their status as text'. For Miller, what is missing from Lejeune's idea of the 'autobiographical contract' is precisely any attention to the relation of gender to genre: by focusing on genre as a category and defining it according to a strict set of rules what inevitably also gets preserved is a masculine genealogy of the subject. What Miller proposes instead is a more generalised commitment on the part of the reader to read differently, to attempt to perceive the different 'inscription of a female subject' across the boundaries of genre. In effect Miller perceives two contradictory dangers which she wants to guard against: one danger is that women's texts will *always* be read as autobiographical whatever their putative genre – here she cites Colette's attack on the male reader who perceives women as only able to write about themselves but we could well add to this many examples from Plath criticism. However, there is also another danger for Miller: that the female autobiographical subject will never be identified – will simply get missed out – in a generically based reading which attempts to be neutral or neuter.[38]

Following Miller's argument, then, the question needing to be asked may be less how autobiographical is *The Bell Jar* or how far are we entitled or enabled to read this novel as fictionalised autobiography than how does this work seek to embody a woman's signature, how does it address the problem of identity, the search through language for the woman's 'proper' name, a name which may not be her legal or legitimate one but her 'own'? Jacqueline Rose has suggested in respect to Plath's pseudonymous authorship of the novel that we view the name Victoria Lucas not in isolation but as one of a series of names – names such as Sandra Peters, Sylvan Hughes and Sadie Peregrine – which Plath played with as alternate possibilities in the course of her writing career; as such, according to Rose it 'reinforces the divisions and differences of the voices in which, formally or generically, she chose to write'.[39] This is interesting since it shifts the discussion away from the name as a written guarantee of identity – a legal signature – which can also, of course, as in the case of a pseudonym, be forged – to writing itself as a form of naming, a play on or with names. 'We are much more than what our own name authorizes us to believe we are', Hélène Cixous has written, directing us to those areas of chance and possibility which surround any assumption of identity.[40] Writing, we could argue, becomes the space where new names can be put into play, where the woman writer can authorise herself as other or more, name herself as author, or even as the author of the author, through the text that she writes.

Significantly all this finds its fictional counterpart in *The Bell Jar* itself. One of the central preoccupations of the novel turns out to be precisely the power of names to bestow identity or to take it away. Twice in the course of the novel the protagonist Esther Greenwood attempts to pass herself off under a pseudonym, renaming herself, with deflationary effect, as Elly Higginbottom. The first time this happens she quite literally diverges from the path she is expected to take, leaping from a taxi after her friend Doreen, at the invitation of a man she doesn't know. The new name is for Esther a barrier placed between her and what is happening, an attempt to ward off contamination, a guarantee that she also exists elsewhere: 'I didn't want anything I said or did that night to be associated with me and my real name and coming from Boston' (p. 12). Yet what begins as protection for Esther ends up reinforcing her feelings of alienation, sealing her into an identity which others take as the 'truth' whilst she melts more and more into the shadows. Disconcertingly even her friend Doreen seems to lose track, as the evening wears on, of the fact Esther is pretending: 'She seemed to think Elly was who I really was by now' (p. 16).

The second time Esther poses as Elly Higginbottom is when she returns home to Boston from New York. Again, it is a casual encounter with a man – this time a sailor – which provokes the impersonation, though with her life disintegrating, the new name and identity now seem momentarily to offer a way out, a fantasised alternative to the burden of individuality. Paradoxically she imagines 'people would take me for what I was' only when she is no longer herself:

> I would be simple Elly Higginbottom, the orphan. People would love me for my sweet, quiet nature. They wouldn't be after me to read books and write long papers on the twins in James Joyce. And one day I might just marry a virile, but tender, garage mechanic and have a big cowy family like Doda Conway. (p. 140)

This dream of acceptance depends on Esther mis-identifying or mis-placing herself since to become acceptable she must recast herself in the very role she has rejected; she must become the woman (or Woman) she despises.

Shortly before this Esther has fantasised about writing a novel. The novel gets no further than the first three sentences before the words collapse, merging again with Esther's confusion and lack of purpose. However, to begin with it had also provided another opportunity for Esther to project herself into a new identity or 'character':

> A feeling of tenderness filled my heart. My heroine would be myself, only in disguise. She would be Elaine. Elaine. I counted the letters on my fingers. There were six letters in Esther, too. It seemed a lucky thing. (pp. 126-7)

There are also, of course, six letters in the name Sylvia. The choice and use of names, this seems to suggest, is a complex strategy: on the one hand names offer linguistic 'cover'; they are dissociated other selves, names for the fictions of identity they help to create; on the other hand names can contain private codes, establish connections however tendentious and arbitrary with other names, hint at the unconscious traces they also help to conceal.

In this instance the 'disguise' briefly enables a moment of tender recognition and must be set against the many violent unmaskings that Esther experiences in the course of the novel. One of the paradoxes that *The Bell Jar* explores is that Esther's relation to others constantly reveals an inner insubstantiality; looking to others for sustenance she finds them already situated inside, eating her away from within. At the *Ladies' Day* banquet Esther, who had 'never eaten out in a proper restaurant' (p. 25) before she came to New York, quite literally attempts to eat her fill, gorging herself on the rich food as if to make up for the 'economy' meals of her childhood. In order to underline the idea of absence Doreen is missing from the feast, leaving an empty place next to Esther, the pocket-mirror on her place card waiting to be filled in by her face. Doreen is the friend who has 'intuition', whose words have already bypassed Esther's flesh, the outer layers of her selfhood, to become 'like a secret voice speaking straight out of my own bones' (p. 7). If Esther at the banquet eats enough for two, it is because her body like her mind is not her own; consumed by someone else's thoughts, she must take ravenously from the outside in order to placate the hunger created inside her.[41]

Whilst she is eating Esther thinks back to a meeting earlier that morning with the editor Jay Cee who had 'unmasked her', so she thinks, by confirming her own 'suspicions' about the hollowness of all her previous achievements (p. 30). In a dialectic where inner and outer seem constantly to change places – where she is dependent on the Other for her identity – Esther characteristically finds herself seen through when she is scrutinised from the outside. Later, poisoned by what she has eaten, Esther vomits violently: 'I thought I was losing my guts and my dinner both' (p. 46). By eliminating her own 'insides', Esther finds relief in also wiping out all trace of the Other. After she has been given an injection Esther is told by a nurse that she will now sleep:

> And the door took her place like a sheet of blank paper, and then a larger sheet of paper took the place of the door, and I drifted towards it and smiled myself to sleep. (pp. 48–9)

Esther, with the closed door blanking out the nurse, who will return later in the person of Doreen, then also blanks out the door, finding safety at last in a space which others cannot gain access to. However, what is also established in the meantime through this image is some kind of relation between food and language, both of which are implicated in a culture and ideology which Esther finds unpalatable. 'I hate technicolor' (p. 43) Esther thinks just before she becomes sick, forced to sit through a film which is a cross between a 'football romance' and *Gone With the Wind* and which luridly enforces its message about the place of 'nice' girls and 'sexy' girls within the structures of heterosexual romance. The magazine *Ladies' Day* which hosts the banquet features 'lush double-page spreads of technicolor meals' (p. 26); the 'spread' that Esther actually eats is the same – comes from the same 'glossy kitchens' (p. 27) – as the food prepared for popular consumption via photographs in the magazine. The image of the blank paper at the moment when Esther lies in her room empty of food and words, suggests an impossible state of purity – a state before her body's inscription in and by culture – which she can only reach through unconsciousness, by becoming blank herself.

The idea of Esther's internal space being already usurped from without is repeated in her relation to events: Esther's characteristic numbness registers her response to a history which has already overwhelmed her, which has invaded her and yet simultaneously escaped her full understanding. This, in some ways, corresponds to D.W. Winnicott's observation that the fear of breakdown is really 'the fear of a breakdown that has already been experienced'; according to Winnicott the subject anxiously anticipates something which already inhabits her, is yet to happen only in the sense that the subject before was 'not there for it to happen to'.[42] The Rosenbergs' execution, the subject of Esther's first words in the novel, seems to register both violence and a traumatised reaction to it at the level of event and symbol. Esther is both possessed by the thought of the Rosenbergs – 'I couldn't get them out of my mind' (p. 1) – and yet unable to acknowledge her feelings. Being 'stupid about executions' (p. 1) carries the conscious meaning of responding in a way which is excessive or inappropriate; at another level, however, Esther is also stupefied, unable to respond at all. Later in the novel when Hilda makes her shocking statement that she's 'so glad they're going to die' (p. 104) it is at first without a context. As the full exchange between Hilda and Esther is gradually revealed what also becomes apparent is that Hilda has stunned Esther into silence, taking Esther's feelings and translating them into her own complete absence of sympathy for the condemned couple. Significantly the imagery through which this scene is represented is of diabolic possession: Hilda reminds Esther of a play where 'the heroine was possessed by a dybbuk, and when the dybbuk spoke from her mouth its voice sounded so cavernous and deep you couldn't tell whether it was a man or a woman' (p. 105). The 'blind cave' behind Hilda's face which Esther sees as the dybbuk's hiding place suggests an inaccessible region out of which emerges words which cannot be placed, can neither be listened to nor related back to their speaker. As Esther faces Hilda, the impossibility of integrating the violence of Hilda's statement (which thoughtlessly repeats the violence of her society) with the blank indifference of Hilda herself also seems to reflect back to Esther her own dissociated response to trauma, the impossibility of her fully assimilating what has occurred.

To begin with mention of the Rosenbergs is put in the context of another 'haunting' event for Esther, her first sight of a 'cadaver' which Buddy Willard, as it turns out among other 'sights', has exposed her to. At the time of her visit, under Buddy's tutelage, to the hospital Esther asserts that 'these cadavers were so unhuman-looking they didn't bother me a bit' (p. 65). Esther must similarly dehumanise her response, turning shock into blandness, when she looks at the preserved foetuses and later watches a woman, drugged and cut by the doctors, painfully giving birth. Coming as the last of these 'clinical' sightings of the body it is not surprising that Buddy's 'educational' display of his genitals to Esther produces little or no response. For Esther all these incidents coincide with another significant event: Buddy's uncovering or unmasking as a 'hypocrite' whose 'purity' has not inhibited him from also having an affair with a waitress. The brutalising of the body which Esther witnesses and her own numbing of response is linked for her – at least chonologically – with the recognition of her designated place as 'nice' or 'sexy' within the same sexual script which she has already observed and which accords only the man the freedom to do what he likes.

Before Esther's most determined and near fatal attempt to commit suicide she visits her father's grave. 'I had a great yearning, lately, to pay my father back for all the years of neglect, and start tending his grave' (p. 175). Who has neglected whom in this scenario, we may ask, where reparation and anger seem intimately allied?[43] Yet if this moment seems to take us back to an earlier crucial event where Esther – as she does with Buddy – 'freezes' her emotions, where complex feelings of disillusionment are similarly linked to an 'unreal' experience of death, it would be a simplification to attempt to trace the origin of Esther's 'trauma' in any straightforward, linear way back to her father's death. For what the novel shows us is that Esther must experience her femininity – her feminine body – within terms of a culture which has already inflicted its violent message on her, where each painful experience of her own – experiences which include an attempted rape, electric shock treatment and a loss of virginity which leaves her almost haemorrhaging to death – seem not just predictable, but already predicted.[44] In these terms we could also give a different meaning to the father's death; for the 'dead father' is in the 'masterful' position of being beyond reach of the anguish and desire that are now invested solely in the daughter's body; he reinforces her physicality by making any identification with him or his knowledge potentially fatal.

Significantly Esther can imagine a different, non-violent, relation to the body – a relation of tenderness – only when she can glimpse alternatives to her own story. This happens on one occasion in hospital, after her breakdown, when, having intruded on Joan and her friend Dee Dee in bed together, she then asks Dr Nolan: '"What does a woman see in a woman that she can't see in a man?"' Dr Nolan's reply which 'shuts her up' is the single word 'tenderness' (p. 231). The novel is very far from offering lesbianism as a 'real' choice as Joan's suicide would seem to demonstrate; however, what this scene suggests is that tenderness or its possibility can only enter the novel as a disruption to Esther's 'normal' thinking about sexuality. The other moment when Esther contemplates tenderness is, as we have seen, when she attempts to writes about herself 'in disguise' as a fictional character and 'a feeling of tenderness' fills her heart (p. 126). Is this the novel, we may ask, that Plath as well as Esther could not write? Can 'tenderness' only figure in a fictive or 'unreal' space, at the very edges of what can be represented? These questions bring us back, I suggest, to other larger questions: not to de Man's question of how the autobiographical can ever be other than 'fictional', but rather the question of what the fiction is attempting to do; what it is attempting to resolve. In Plath's case, her novel – her fiction – seems to repeat the very dilemma she faced as a writer, trying to project her 'self' into writing. For however hard she may try to imagine otherwise, Esther repeatedly discovers that her gendered body is already commodified, violently appropriated, beyond her control. It would have been no comfort to Plath, of course, to know how accurately she uncovered in her novel the difficulty of creating fictions which did not simply repeat her own culture's violence; nor how hauntingly she could even be said in this novel to have predicted her own reification as cultural myth: the process by which her 'self', appropriated as commodity, would be used to sell her books.

CHAPTER SIX

Feminist autobiography: the personal and the political

In an interview by her friend and fellow poet Adrienne Rich, which was originally published in *Signs* in 1981, Audre Lorde outlined, mingling discursive with autobiographical writing, her theory of poetry.[1] For Lorde, writing about poetry is almost of necessity 'unfinished', part of a process of thinking – a 'progression' – which she as yet does not know the end of (p. 81). Turning quickly to her own 'experience' Lorde describes the way throughout her life she 'kept' herself through feeling, through being profoundly distrustful of how language codifies and reifies knowledge. Significantly, she claims that it was from her mother that she learned a different means of non-verbal communication, a respect for the information which could pass intuitively between people. Poetry becomes a way of mediating this other knowledge, a mysterious process which flouts the rules of grammar and syntax, almost too precious, too close to herself, to be given written form at all. 'Like a translation into this poem that already existed of something you knew in a preverbal way', Rich offers, paraphrasing or 'translating' Lorde (p. 82). This is a statement to which Lorde readily assents.

This moment when Rich 'intuits' Lorde, correctly interpreting her meaning, in many ways characterises the interview. Though it *is* an interview and not a dialogue – Rich's role is to facilitate responses by Lorde who remains the subject of the piece – there is an assumption of mutuality and agreement between them, the sense of a conversation between friends which has been going on before the interview and which extends beyond its frame. Lorde, indeed, describes their conversations as so much a part of her inner life that they cross the boundary between the real and the imaginary, occurring in a symbolic 'space' beyond their immediate personalities:

> Adrienne, in my journals I have a lot of pieces of conversations that I'm having with you in my head. I'll be having a conversation with you and I'll put it in my journal because stereotypically or symbolically these conversations occur in a space of Black woman/white woman where it's beyond Adrienne and Audre, almost as if we're two voices. (p. 103)

At this point, however, Rich objects, interrupting the flow of empathy between them; what she asks for, resisting her elision in Lorde's speech, is a clearer distinction between 'the conversations you have in your head' and 'the conversations we're having on this earth'. She then goes on to dispute how Lorde has 'internalised' a previous conversation that they have had, refusing the role that Lorde ascribed to her of being rational, and by implication, unemotional or unintuitive:

> One of the crosses I've borne all my life is being told that I'm rational, logical, cool – I am not cool, and I'm not rational and logical in that icy sense. But there's a way in which, trying to translate from your experience to mine, I do need to hear chapter and verse from time to time. I'm afraid of it all slipping away into: 'Ah, yes, I understand you.' . . . So if I ask for documentation, it's because I take seriously the spaces between us that difference has created, that racism has created. (p. 104)

The interview has here shifted its ground, dramatically confronting the problem of the differences *between* women, and of whether these can be articulated in a mode which collapses the distance between them. Rich is in effect caught in a double-bind for she can only define her difference by adopting that other language – a rational language – by taking up a subject position which seems to be outside the mutual space of their shared discourse.

This moment of conflict and contradiction could be understood in terms of the intervention of history into the intimate scene of the two women's encounter. Not only do Rich and Lorde replay here an earlier instance of unresolved difficulty between them, they also acknowledge their differences in terms of race. The history of racism and the different positions they occupy within that history becomes the inescapable context for their interraction; their historically determined identities as Black and White enters their relation in ways they cannot altogether control. At the same time, however, it may also be possible for us to reverse this, to see this interview as – at least in part – creating its own time and space, existing in terms of a malleable or fluid topography where positions are not already fixed: in this sense the 'face-to-face' meeting between the two women enables them also to resite their differences, reframe them, by allowing them to exist *within* the space of their intimate exchange. Much as we can think of the psychoanalytic encounter as reorienting the relation of past to present, as creating a setting or a scene in which the subject can produce herself differently, can 'be' in a different relation to the 'other' and to language, so this interview could be seen as making available a different space between the two women, a dynamic space which connects whatever they say not just to the past, to the already said, but also to each other in the here and now. Can opposites and differences become part of a process of exchange? What might it mean to speak the differences *between* women? These are the questions which this interview raises and they are crucial questions in thinking about a feminist politics of the subject. What history determines, so Rich and Lorde suggest between them, could be open to change if we attend to its particularity and discreteness – its volatility – in the present.

In her book, *Feminism and Psychoanalysis: The Daughter's Seduction*, Jane Gallop sees the dramatic potential – a scenario of positions and roles – in the differences between the two feminist theorists Luce Irigaray and Julia Kristeva.[2] Referring to an early essay by Irigaray, 'And the One Does Not Stir without The Other', Gallop describes the way Irigaray speaks her impassioned plea for separateness to the mother, thus claiming a discursive position for herself as daughter. Ironically, however – by that same mode of address – she also confirms the mother in her role as the silent receiver of the child's discourse, as the one who has power to control or change the relationship yet who has no power to speak for her own part.[3] If Irigaray speaks from the position of daughter then Kristeva, according to Gallop, assumes the power to speak from the place of the mother.[4] However, this is in many ways a questionable power, since though Kristeva in her writings posits the possibility of a maternal 'I', she also says that maternity happens in a space where no one is present to signify what is going on: '"It happens but I'm not there"'.[5] The maternal body, according to Kristeva, exists outside the the socio-symbolic contract, on the threshold between nature and culture. The mother who speaks, therefore, is the 'phallic mother', the mother fantasised from the side of the symbolic as subject, as able to fill the spaces which would otherwise be unrepresentable. What is the difference, we may ask, between Irigaray's projection on to the mother of a power which the daughter does not possess herself and Kristeva's 'phallic mother' whose power derives from the ascription to her of a symbolic status which *in reality* she does not have? Do both have to struggle in the end with the difficulty of separating the female subject from phallocentric definitions of maternity? Does the daughter's collapse into the mother arise from the impossibility of conceiving of a female subject on any other terms?

This is precisely the point that Gallop is making and the danger for her – despite its attractions – of any neat configuration which places Irigaray and Kristeva on either side of the mother–daughter relationship. Indeed it may be the very symmetry of that relation which poses the problems, assuming a clarity and fixity that effaces a much more complex relation between two women. Gallop suggests that the category of mother neither defines their relation nor can it be completely excluded from it. 'The relation to the other woman only approaches its full complexity with some recognition that the 'other woman' as well as oneself is and is not 'Mother'.[6] This is why, in this part of her book, despite her attention to both theorists, Gallop leans towards Kristeva, seeing her as providing a model of how to exercise power and criticise it, to be both mother and daughter, to take on a phallic position and simultaneously expose its fraudulence. A relation to the other – moving on from Irigaray to Kristeva – does not prevent mobility, rather it becomes a way of engendering it: 'A permanent alternation: never one without the other.'[7]

However, in her writing since the essay that Gallop uses to such good effect Irigaray has not stayed still – nor have interpretations of her work.[8] We may now be in a better position to hear Irigaray differently and through her to hear the speech between women differently, as a potential discourse which need not rely for its definition and understanding on a reference to the same. Irigaray's writing in this sense could be read as intervening *between* what is and what is yet to be, attempting to create a new symbolic space where none was thought to exist. Kristeva envisages an oscillation between different positions which nevertheless leaves those positions theoretically in place: the maternal cannot be directly spoken of except across the gap – the experience of loss that must be undergone in order for the subject to enter the symbolic – which forever separates language from the mother's body. Irigaray's writing, however, attempts to imagine how women, instead of silently mediating the relation between nature or the body and language for men, might create the possibility of a symbolic exchange between themselves. Language, in Irigaray's view, produces a paralysis in women because it is not their own to put into play; they borrow and imitate; they become subjects only in the manner of men. Irigaray's work is aimed towards a different future. 'The fact that female intelligence is still *silent* surely means that there are *movements* that must still be set free.'[9] The mother–daughter relation is not *inevitably* suffocating, airless, caught, in a 'distanceless proximity';[10] this is so only because at the moment there is no symbolic process to account for it, there are no words between women. We have no difficulty, so Irigaray argues, in thinking about relations of merging and fusion – and we could add theorists, of which the pre-eminent is Kristeva, have in recent years addressed very fully the pre-oedipal or semiotic – what has not been achieved is 'a different interpretation of what is in play in these fusional relations'.[11] Everything has to take place 'in some deadly immediacy',[12] 'before speech intervenes'[13] because there is no 'imaginary or symbolic ground' recognised '"on the side of women"'.[14] For Irigaray, women are not just subjects of the symbolic but social subjects with their own singular history which has not been accorded symbolic recognition. For this reason she is critical of psychoanalytic theory as laying down a priori laws, of its imperialistic unconscious to which everyone must become subject; theory should rather be responsive to changing discourses, to its own connection to history, to what is potential or 'remains to be discovered, especially the future in the past'.[15] In terms of the themes of this book – and the dual claims of autobiography and theory – theory might be seen as constructing a mode of understanding which can offer a critique of common sense, of whatever becomes accepted as simply 'true', which is and can never be complete, whilst autobiography, in its historical materiality, could be seen as productive of a specificity, an unexpectedness or excess, never totally explicable in terms of theory. We have come back to Kristeva's notion of how different positions might be used to interrogate each other but with a different understanding of what might be at stake politically and an awareness of how carefully differentiated and how flexible the space between them could be. In terms of imagining a relation in which we could hold the two theorists who have criss-crossed their way through this book, it may be important that we are able to hear one without necessarily cancelling out the other.

The difficulty of saying we

In 1977 Adrienne Rich published her influential and important analysis of motherhood, *Of Woman Born: Motherhood as Experience and Institution.*[16] Ten years later, on the event of its republication, she returned to it in order to add a new Introduction, aware that she as subject and thinker had in the meantime changed. Rich, thinking back to the writing of the book, dates its inception to 1972, 'some four or five years into a new politicization of women' when there was 'virtually nothing being written on motherhood as an issue'.[17] The challenge of the book was to use the 'concrete and particular experiences of women' but also to write about motherhood 'in a social context, as embedded in a political institution'. This weaving together of the personal and the political was precisely what defined it as 'feminist'. In 1986, however, Rich is dissatisfied with how this *relation* between the personal and the political has come to mean the personal for its own sake and the tension or difference between the two terms lost:

> *Of Woman Born* was both praised and attacked for what was sometimes seen as its odd-fangled approach: personal testimony mingled with research and theory which derived from both. But this approach never seemed odd to me in the writing. What seems odd is the absentee author, the writer who lays down speculations, theories, facts, and fantasies without any personal grounding. On the other hand, I have felt recently that the late 1960s Women's Liberation thesis that 'the personal is political' (which helped to release this book into being) has been overlaid by a New Age blur

of the personal-for-its-own-sake, as if 'the personal is good' had become the corollary and the thesis forgotten.

She goes on to quote from Audre Lorde's poem 'There Are No Honest Poems About Dead Women' which asks 'What do we want from each other/after we have told our stories'. The problem for Rich is where feminism is going and it is a problem which engages precisely the language of space and movement:

> The question of what we do want beyond a 'safe space' is crucial to the differences between the individualistic telling with no place to go and a collective movement to empower women.

An 'individualistic telling' runs the risk of being unable to imagine a place other than its own, of returning to the same, 'safe place', which seems connected to the fantasised pre-oedipal maternal body, rather than imagining different times and places. As a collective movement feminism aims to change the social and symbolic status of women but it can never arrive where it thinks – indeed its own project is ceaselessly displaced by, in Rich's terms, 'the differences between' the individual and the collective or the plural histories which 'we' contain. The specificity of history – of histories – unsettles feminism's own urge towards ideological and theoretical abstraction. In this sense – in its necessary resistance to, or suspicion of, its own generalisations about women – feminism can never be totally at home with itself.

For Rich, what she perceives, ten years on, as having changed the terrain of her original argument is the success of 'a vigorous and widespread women's health-care movement', which in the wake of women's testimony about their abuse, worked towards the creation of new practices and institutions which could serve women's needs. What, therefore, lies beyond the 'individualistic telling' for Rich is activism, the purposeful drive towards social change. Yet what Rich also sees is that change has been limited – that it has affected the lives of poor or Chichana or Black or lesbian women (and here Rich is also limiting her frame of reference to the USA) in only minor ways – also that focused on particular issues around reproduction such changes can be incorporated, contained, with a minimum of disturbance to an existing hierarchy of gender relations. Rich's act of re-vision involves her, then, in rethinking the limits of the emancipatory history – the linear, progressive project – which feminism itself helped to frame. It is not just that feminism, as it was conceived in the 1970s, came up against certain blocks but that those limitations, occlusions, were there within it from the start.

No where is this more forcibly and painfully felt in this Introduction than when Rich surveys her own blind spots. Pointing particularly to her chapter on 'Motherhood and Daughterhood', she recognises that whilst she did not confine herself solely to materials drawn from a white, middle-class Anglo-Saxon tradition, this tradition of female or feminist writing did, nevertheless, provide 'the lens for viewing her subject', thus distorting her argument and even rendering the representation of her own experience partial or inadequate. Having acknowledged in her original text that she was cared for by a Black nurse, Rich can now see that she also framed that relationship in terms of a generalised mother–daughter relationship and 'glided over' 'the concrete system within which Black women have had to nurture the oppressor's children'. Rich cites 'a rich literature by Afro- and Caribbean-American women, and more and more by American Indian, Asian American, Latin' which has challenged the general applicability of the concepts through which early (white) feminism thought itself. Accordingly the mother–daughter bond, at the heart of Rich's concerns, is unable, in this rereading, to transcend 'wide variations of culture and history'.

Rich's reassessment follows recent trends in feminism whereby the continuity and general availability of its own categories of thought are put into question: the different and heterogeneous perspectives of Black women, other women of colour, working-class women, it has been argued, cannot simply be absorbed into the terms of a debate, rooted in White Western history, where the individualism securing masculine identity and which feminism has struggled against, is reasserted on the side of women. 'Women' itself, therefore, has become a problematic term within feminism, suggesting a stability or even a naturalness around the notion of gender which has never really been the case. For Denise Riley, once the term is recognised as being both historically and culturally variable, it must be radically reformulated: '"Women" is a volatile collectivity in which female persons can be very differently positioned so that the apparent continuity of the subject of "women" isn't to be relied on.'[18] For Donna Harraway, too, the term has become 'elusive': 'There is nothing about being "female" that naturally binds women.'[19]

This struggle around the terms of women's identity or identification also marks Rich's passage as autobiographical subject within her essays. Just as she returned to *Of Women Born* from a new or different place, so she has revised, in her essays written in the 1980s, how she chooses to situate herself. In her famous essay, 'When We Dead Awaken: Writing as Re-Vision', first given as a talk in 1971, she turns to herself in what now seems a familiar autobiographical gesture as both illustration and continuation of her argument about the difficulties confronting the woman writer.[20] The story that she tells establishes a trajectory for her life and career in terms of the emergence of a unified and authentic self. To begin with, so she saw it, split between the seemingly mutually exclusive identities of poet and woman, she could only install herself in discourse by repeating the masculine gesture of objectifying herself as Woman: 'I hadn't found the courage . . . to use the pronoun "I" – the woman in the poem is always "she" (p. 45). Of a later poem, which in the essay is used to mark the end or culmination of her journey, she comments triumphantly: 'At last the woman in the poem and the woman writing the poem become the same person' (p. 47). This narrative effects a powerful reversal of the negative identification of woman in Western discourse into a positive one, but it could also be said to lead to an impasse, for women are still locked into the same system of meaning, reabsorbed within a wholeness which recognises no 'other' identities, no otherness within the concept of identity. At the end of her essay Rich, assuming a continuity between her 'self' and other women, easily accomplishes a shift from autobiographical exploration to the affirmation of a shared female consciousness. Detecting, as she believes, a new generation of woman poet, she eulogises how 'women are speaking to and of women in these poems, out of a newly released courage to name, to love each other, to share risk and grief and celebration' (p. 49).

What is at issue is Rich's own ideological 'placing' but this can also be thought about, reversing figure and ground, in terms of how space is being imagined. As Gillian Rose has pointed out, 'the white bourgeois heterosexual masculinist theorist . . . claims to see everywhere from nowhere, because all the contamination of specificity has been expelled from his position.'[21] Within this discourse space as reality, as materiality, is both erased and endlessly converted into metaphor; the white masculine subject's imperialism or violent territorialism is thus rendered invisible; space becomes synonymous with the operations of mind, refigured in terms of the bounded and autonomous space of a room in which the subject can meditate quietly on himself.[22] The difficulty for the female subject is then both to claim a 'room of her own' – a space for her own subjectivity – without getting trapped in the same territorial logic.[23] Even the attempt to think beyond the hegemonic space of the masculine subject – the powerful desire for, as Rich puts it, 'a new space on the boundaries of patriarchy' (p. 49) – can end up, caught in the same binary system of inclusion and exclusion, reinforcing the structures it opposes. The 'whole new psychic geography' that Rich envisages as both 'challenge and promise' (p. 35) for the woman writer, is predicated on an idea or an ideal of wholeness, a euphoric vision which obscures the recognition of the other spaces, not beyond patriarchy, but within it which patriarchy must then deny or cover over in order to maintain its own wholeness.

'How to keep Utopia in its place?' Elizabeth Weed has asked, a complex and ambiguous question which seems to situate utopia on both sides of the nowhere/somewhere, imaginary/real divide. The same could be said of her notion of an 'interim utopia', a conjunction of words which links an ideal, unrealisable future to what might be possible in the present.[23] How might we imagine space differently? Is there room in the interstices for what we do not know or do no know yet, a 'blank part of the text', in Gayatri Spivak's words, 'given over to the future'?[24] Utopia, invoked as a space of difference, perhaps need not be relegated to an impossible exterior, but could be thought about as a future anterior, that folding of the future into the present or the past, contained in the formulation, 'what will have been'; not somewhere we can ever return to or arrive at – never somewhere that can be planned or predicted or retreated to – but an opening up of present parameters towards change. According to Elizabeth Grosz, who takes the point from Irigaray, 'masculine modes of thought' have disavowed their relation to space because they 'have obliterated the debt they owe to the most primordial of all spaces, the maternal space from which all subjects emerge'.[25] This presents feminism with a twofold task: to disrupt the 'clean' spaces of masculine thought with the evidence of its own material or maternal origins but also to begin to symbolise the female subject's own relation to space in terms other than as the support – container, matter or unfathomable spatiality – for masculine self-representations. This second – utopian – movement is important and it means that though Irigaray and the feminist thinkers she has inspired, would seem to adopt the language of essentialism in order to challenge masculine disavowals – to present space as origin or material essence – this is also the way through to somewhere else. According to Naomi Schor, whilst male philosophers, 'are free because of their founding exclusion of the maternal– feminine to deny their own essentialism', Irigaray is 'obliged not only to pass through essentialism but to speak its language'.[26] For Schor, space as place or essence needs to be linked to movement: it needs to be thought about not as a 'goal' so much as a moment of becoming.[27] Indeed in order neither to deny the old binaries – which would simply cede universalism to masculine thought – nor get trapped in her (no) place within them, the female subject requires such a new conjuction of space and movement: a notion of boundaries which are not fixed, which do not prevent one side being thought about as being permeated by, absorbing or moving towards the other. 'Boundaries', Elizabeth Grosz suggests – and it is through such formulations that new spaces are beginning to be tracked for the female subject – 'do not so much define the routes of passage; it is movement that defines and constitutes boundaries'.[28]

In the early 1980s, when Rich returned to the autobiographical essay form, it is with an understanding of how 'location' has become a key and problematic term within feminism. Her first move, then, is to introduce a sense of real geographical space rather separating it as a term, or metaphor from its 'ground'. In 'Blood, Bread, and Poetry: The Location of the Poet', she begins with a statement of both a moment and a place: 'The Miami airport, summer 1983.'[29] The occasion is an imminent visit to Nicaragua – a crossing of 'real' geographical borders – but it also becomes the scene of a meeting, a 'chance' remark which then provokes her reflections on geographical and cultural difference: 'A North American woman says to me, "You'll love Nicaragua: Everyone there is a poet." I've thought many times of that remark, both while there and since returning home' (p. 167). This seemingly 'well-meant' pleasantry carries with it a weight of assumption about poetry, about politics but most of all about the speaker's own capacity to see and judge across national and cultural difference, to experience her own position as 'unmarked'. It is this 'delusion' that 'white is at the center' (p. 183) that Rich is exposing in her essay, along with the need for herself and other (white) women 'to admit and explore our cultural identities, our national identities' (p. 183). 'As a lesbian-feminist poet and writer' she writes 'I need to understand how this location affects me, along with the realities of blood and bread within this nation' (p. 183).

Rich is here attempting to arrive at an understanding of her own location as a speaking subject – of how 'location' and 'position' are implicated in each other as geographical and ideological placings. This understanding, despite the peremptory and unequivocal sense of 'need', seems to depend as much on 'affect', on the body, as it does on a (self) conscious knowledge. In her essay, 'Notes Towards a Politics of Location', Rich explores more fully the difficulty of ever fully understanding one's' 'location', which is never, after all, static and stable but dependent on numerous 'crossings'. In this essay no one position is ever fully coincident with 'her', can ever transcend the different places she occupies; instead the essay is a series of 'notes' without 'absolute conclusions' which move between reminiscence, reflection, exhortation, quotation, mingling different styles of discourse and different voices. Writing, then, is a series of beginnings, dependent on the specificity of place and moment: Rich draws attention to the way 'she' is impinged on by the immediacy of her surroundings – not simply absorbed in a place of self-reflective study. These 'happenings' then become part of the 'material' of her writing:

> Beginning to write, then getting up. Stopped by the movements of a huge early bumblebee which has somehow gotten inside this house and is reeling, bumping, stunning itself against windowpanes and sills . . .
> And I, too, have been bumping my way against glassy panes, falling half-stunned, gathering myself up and crawling, then again taking off, searching. (p. 211)

Rich translates into metaphor what begins as chance, constructing herself through the efffort to draw meaning out of both the past and the present.

For Rich this attention to specificity is also part of an acknowledgement that she can no longer assume a position of universality: 'A few years ago I would have spoken of the common oppression of women.' She goes on:

> I would have spoken these words as a feminist who 'happened' to be
> a white United States citizen . . . quoting without second thought
> Virginia Woolf's statement in *Three Guineas* that 'as a woman I have
> no country. As a woman my country is the whole world.' (p. 211)

In 1984 she recognises the 'faceless, raceless, classless category of
"all women"' as a creation of 'white Western self-centredness' and
acknowledges that much of feminist theorising has been based on
'lived experience' which has been 'thoughtlessly white' (p. 219). For
Rich, the struggle is now to give up certain privileges and
certainties, without also abandoning the ethical basis of feminism:
'These notes are the marks of a struggle to keep moving, a struggle
for accountability' (p. 211). Seeing herself as moving between
provisional or temporary contexts – indeed seeing her 'self' as
constructed and determined by them – does not, however, absolve
her from responsibility for her political situation as a White
American, and Rich in this essay is putting together two seemingly
different senses of 'chance', the 'chance' which denotes the
randomness and fragmentation which undermines the stability of
the speaking subject and his or her claim to transcendence and the
'chance' which 'situates' one in a particular history, a particular
place and time which is one's 'own'. Movement, then, as Rich is
invoking it, is close to the idea of movement described by Grosz
above, movement as a necessary part of defining where one is. It
does not mean slipperiness or lack of enagagement or indifference:
it does not substitute a presumed neutrality or objectivity with the
position of having no position, no 'self' to hold to account. There
is still the need, as Gayatri Spivak puts it, to '"recognize" oneself
as an instantiation of historical and psychosexual narratives that one
can piece together however fragmentarily': to deconstruct identity
but on the other hand not to refuse it as responsibility or strategy
or choice.[30]

Rich is here confronting what has been one of the most difficult
and intractable problems within contemporary feminism: the way
and the terms on which feminism, once it has recognised its own
implication in the 'master' narratives of liberal humanism, can lay
claim to the categories of agency and representativeness which
may be necessary for political action or strategy; how feminism
can situate itself within deconstructive practices – how it can
recognise the fragmentation and destabilisation of the subject, of

identity – without effacing its own struggle for recognition. Does the acknowledgement of the differences between women undermine a feminist politics, making it impossible to generalise, to assert or analyse how women are oppresed as a sex? Who does 'feminism' represent? Where and for whom do I speak 'as a feminist'? These are the questions that come together when Rich describes in this essay – retaining a sense of both discomfort and uncertainty – the dangers of 'speaking for others':

> The difficulty of saying I – a phrase from the East German novelist Christa Wolf. But once having said it, as we realize the necessity to go further, isn't there a difficulty of saying 'we'? You cannot speak for me. I cannot speak for us. Two thoughts: there is no collective movement that speaks for each of us all the way through.
> And so even ordinary pronouns become a political problem. (p. 224)

The difficulty of saying I, the problem she explored in 'When We Dead Awaken' has changed into a different political problem with ordinary pronouns, or a political problem with different pronouns: now the difficulty for Rich is saying 'we'. Feminism has in the past presumed to 'speak for'; it has not recognised the problem of connecting 'I' to we or seen how its representations of 'women' involved both privilege and exclusion. Rich 'ends' her essay by returning to this same point, with no expectation of either answer or closure: 'Once again: Who is we?/This is the end of these notes, but it is not an ending' (p. 231). This 'conclusion' involves Rich in a stance where none of the conflicts she has identified are resolved yet neither does she retreat or 'shrink' from her ethical and political 'responsibility' as a feminist. Addressing this same problem of speaking for others, Linda Alcoff has similarly refused a polarised position, the either/or of binary thinking: 'To say that location *bears* on meaning and truth is not the same as saying that location *determines* meaning and truth'; and earlier in the same essay: 'A *partial* loss of control does not entail a *complete* loss of accountability.'[31] What Alcoff argues is that the problem of speaking for others is not just a political problem but a problem which 'exists in the very structure of discursive practices'.[32] There is no absolute answer, therefore, and no position of neutrality outside: all that is possible, as Alcoff argues and Rich demonstrates, is the careful tracking of the intersection of location and meaning as it bears on both oneself and others:

> There is no neutral place to stand free and clear in which one's words do not prescriptively affect or mediate the experience of others, nor is there a way to decisively demarcate a boundary between one's location and all others . . . We are collectively caught in an intricate, delicate web in which each action I take, discursive or otherwise pulls on, breaks off, or maintains the tension in many strands of a web in which others find themselves moving also.[33]

My landscape or hers

On the basis of her early – and at the time pioneering – essays Rich, as feminist theorist, has been categorised unfavourably in recent times as a radical feminist or as a 'cultural feminist', whose work is informed by crude and redundant ideas about 'women's experience' and the relation of identity to discourse.[34] Yet the essays in her collection, *Of Blood Bread and Poetry*, have often been cited by Anglo-American critics, who, working within the French tradition, have read her later fragmentation of subjecthood in the context of Barthes and Derrida.[35] Does Rich as a writer pose particular problems of 'placing'? Or have we yet to develop ways of reading the history of feminism which can take account of how the feminist subject moves through it, representing different 'moments' on the way?

For Elizabeth Weed the problem is one of categorisation itself. 'Feminism', she argues 'is not a simple terrain divided into the liberal-humanist versus the theoretical-radical'; rather the categories 'cross one another and overlap in multiple and sometimes unpredictable ways.'[36] Moreover what a historical reading of feminism may unwittingly impose is precisely that teleological structuring of thought that feminism has struggled against, a narrative of progress or development which sees it moving ever closer to the goal of 'truth'. What might it mean to think of overlapping boundaries between the past, present and future? Of ideas which are not static but capable of multiple and different interpretations at different times? What might there be yet to be discovered of the past in the future or even the future in the past?

Shoshana Felman, as we have seen in the Introduction, suggests one such approach to Rich, when, returning to 'When We Dead

Awaken: Writing as Re-Vision' she perceives a moment of hesitation in Rich's text, a moment of critique and doubt interposing itself, just as Rich seeks for authenticity in her 'self' and her own experience. What Felman does is to make us aware of a hiatus or gap in the text, another story which is not the one that Rich expressly tells, but which resists a unitary discourse, its assimilation into a single representation of 'self'.[37] Jane Gallop is equally provocative when she places *Of Woman Born* alongside Barthes' autobiography, *Roland Barthes par Roland Barthes*, two books published within a year of each other, which both according to Gallop, in different ways, 'refuse to respect the separation between objectivity and subjectivity', mixing autobiography with theory and scholarship.[38] For Gallop, an American pursuing French studies, these two books, unrelated to each other except coincidentally and representing different poles of her own intellectual life, assumed an imaginative connection to each other. In the life of the reader – as Gallop suggests – different ideas can traverse each other, strange conjunctions can be made: reading one book – and where and when we read it – may make a difference to how we read another.

It is with these notions of differences – differences that disturb or escape our conscious placing of texts – that I want to return briefly to Adrienne Rich's chapter on 'Motherhood and Daughterhood' in *Of Woman Born*, the chapter with which Rich herself expressed most dissatisfaction when she wrote her new Introduction. Yet Rich's own 'resistance' – in the sense that Felman uses that term as what refuses to fit in with the conscious ideology of a text – is equally apparent in this chapter itself, not only in the way autobiographical and theoretical discourse create internal dissonances or differences, can never merge with each other, but in the way another story – the story of the Other – is always implicated in the story that she tells. Addressing the relation of mothers and daughters, Rich speaks from either position but never fuses (or confuses) them: desiring to recover the blissful, pre-oedipal fusion with the mother's body or voicing the absence of symbolic representations of the relationship, its cultural validation in myth and literature, Rich in fact does something more complicated than either: she begins to explore the difference *between* the two points of view which can never simply be overcome, the necessity for 'double vision' (p. 225), for both sides, for the way the mother, as well as the daughter has a different story to tell.

To begin with Rich, hesitating to embark on this particular part of her book, inscribes her relation to her mother through the difficulty of writing about it:

> A folder lies open beside me as I start to write, spilling out references and quotations, all relevant probably, but none of which can help me to begin. This is the core of my book, and I enter it as a woman who, born between her mother's legs, has time after time and in different ways tried to return to her mother, to repossess her and be repossessed by her, to find the mutual confirmation from and with another woman that daughters and mothers alike hunger for, pull away from, make possible or impossible for each other. (p. 218)

Rich suggests a disjunction between writing and the body which is complex and which exceeds her 'conscious' meaning. Entering her book 'as a woman' who seeks to 'repossess' her intimate relationship with her mother is, of course, precisely what her positioning within language and the symbolic disallows. To enter into writing – to say 'I' – is also to experience the loss of that primordial closeness to the mother's body. How then to return to the mother except across the substitutions of language which intervene between them? 'As a woman' also implies 'like a woman', that is the metonymic displacement of language away from an origin. In a sense the overflowing folder of writing, the writing which cannot be contained and which Rich discards in order to enter her book in a more 'bodily' way, is suggestive of the semiotic, the chaotic scraps and debris which must be repressed in order for 'I' to begin. The implication is, of course, that Rich must turn away from other authorities in order to turn inwards to her own unexplored core. Yet Rich's writing, in this chapter and elsewhere in the book, though it moves continually between autobiography and theory, allowing her 'self' to rest in neither, is orderly and clear: 'she' is situated within the symbolic and does not attempt, stylistically, to dissolve, transgress or exceed it. For Rich, the acknowledgement of desire or 'need' for the mother, the daughter's yearning, which breaks down the unity of the rational, autonomous subject never simply replaces 'understanding', the ability to maintain a critical distance (p. 225). The return to the mother that Rich desires and idealises is located externally as well as internally:

she searches for her outside as well as inside herself, for a mother who exists as a social subject and not just the object of her desire.

'It is hard to write about my own mother', Rich confesses (p. 221). What makes the story difficult to tell for Rich is not only her entanglement with her mother but also her separateness. Their stories are inevitably not the same story, cannot be collapsed into one. 'Whatever I write, it is my story I am telling, my version of the past. If she were to tell her own story other landscapes would be revealed' (p. 221). She cannot simply impose or superimpose her story on her mother's: her mother is more or other than her mother, inhabiting a different 'landscape'. For Rich the mother becomes more fully 'known', not through her recovering her feelings as a daughter – the anger and the pain of her mother's lack of nurture – but through being able to identify with her from the position of mother herself:

> Beneath the 'numbness' that she has since told me she experienced at that time, I can imagine the guilt of Everymother, because I have known it myself.
> But I did not know it yet. And it is difficult for me to write of my mother now, because I have known it too well. I struggle to describe what it felt like to be her daughter, but I find myself divided, slipping under her skin; a part of me identifies too much with her. (pp. 225–6)

Identifying 'too much' is very different, of course, from fusing with her, from experiencing that bodily and emotional fulfilment with the mother which is the daughter's fantasy; it is to recognise the difference between the positions of mother and daughter: being in the place of the mother is to see, too, how far she is from where the daughter thought she was.

In the last section of the chapter, when Rich begins to recover her memories of her 'Black mother', she writes only as a daughter: as she later acknowledged, this involved a failure to 'see' from the perspective of the Black woman, who must for social and economic reasons, undertake the care of White children. Rich's purpose – as it is throughout the chapter – is to address what is hidden, forgotten or repressed by patriarchy: the woman who is denigrated, forgotten, abjected on account of her sex and her race is also the mother and Rich perceives her own and other women's implication in a culture which is built on 'the double silence of sexism and racism' (p. 255). Yet by putting the other woman in the place of the mother, Rich collapses the distinction that she has held so painstakingly throughout the chapter, that the mother is also another woman. In order to be represented as a social subject – and Rich in a sense 'knows' what she later discovers – she must first be allowed to exist in a place other than the place of the mother.

Audre Lorde published her autobiography, *Zami: A New Spelling of My Name*, in 1982.[39] Often situated together as belonging to the same moment of feminism, Rich and Lorde, as we saw at the beginning of this chapter, also speak across differences of race. Lorde called her autobiography a 'biomythography' and this in a sense provides a key to the 'different' way she is employing the genre. Whilst Rich uses autobiography to open up another space within her theoretical writing, to hold each discourse at a distance from the other, Lorde is attempting to create a new myth for her 'self', to put her own act of self-creation at the centre, to incorporate the other into her 'wholeness'. However, where Lorde starts from is a position of difference, exiled from the cultural centrality that Rich can in many ways take for granted. Lorde's text works to resite many of the painful alienations that she experiences as 'Black and foreign and female' (p. 17) in terms of a new myth of connectedness. For Lorde her 'radical feminism' becomes a fiction of unity and 'wholeness' founded on the reality of the differences between women:

> *Being women together was not enough. We were different. Being gay-girls together was not enough. We were different. Being Black together was not enough. We were different. Being Black women together was not enough. We were different. Being Black dykes together was not enough. We were different.* (p. 226)

Difference attends every grouping, every connection, suggesting the instability and mobility of identity or identities. The differences of which 'we' are the subject and which creates alliances also forges divisions: the apparent stability of 'we' in fact covers multiple subject positions.

Lorde attempts to create a home through the writing of her autobiography, to recreate in terms of language and metaphor the home she is exiled from. The term 'home', however, far from signifying one place moves in a complicated way between reality and myth. The geographical place that her mother calls home, the

Caribbean island of Carriacou, is already as Lorde encounters it, a myth, an elsewhere, which opens up the boundaries of the present:

> Once home was a far way off, a place I had never been to but knew well out of my mother's mouth . . . This now, here, was a space, some temporary abode, never to be considered forever nor totally binding nor defining, no matter how much it commanded in energy and attention. For if we lived correctly and with frugality, looked both ways before crossing the street, then someday we would arrive back in the sweet place, back *home*. (p. 13)

The mother's desire for home becomes the daughter's desire and then becomes inseparable from the daughter's desire for the mother and for other women. The mother's 'landscape' is mapped on to her body and on to the body of the women she loves. '*My body, a living representation of other life older longer wiser. The mountains and valleys, trees, rocks. Sand and flowers and water and stone. Made in earth*' (p. 7). The 'naturalising' of the body – the essentialism of this movement towards 'natural' imagery in the prologue – exists, however, alongside Lorde's careful and detailed mapping of differences. So the desire for the mother, the nostalgia for the pre-oedipal fusion with her body, which Lorde tries to recover through her sexual relationships with other women, exists alongside her understanding of her mother's life as an immigrant in Harlem in the 1950s, and her struggles with racisim and poverty. Lorde produces the details of her mother's and her own life in terms of metaphors of desire: she attempts to find a 'maternal' language which can express feminine desire. The economy of metaphor collapses distinctions, fuses times and places: the mother returns in the resonances of language. However, this desire to connect and incorporate, to find a mythic home, exists beside the other documentary aspect of the autobiography, which maps the complexities of the social subject existing in a particular time and place, and for whom there is no home. The ending provides a 'homecoming' and a sense of 'wholeness' in terms of images: it also concludes with a 'real' parting, a separation.

The differences inscribed by Lorde and Rich within their autobiographical writing complicates the feminist ideology they are often seen to represent. Their attention to difference, however, is also different – it is also produced by and expresses their differences from each other. Yet to think of these differences is not to hold them in a configuration which does not also allow for movement. The use of autobiography by Lorde and Rich, the way auto-biography can begin to map the specificity of difference, opens up the space between, makes it also a space mediated and traversed by language. The words that begin to exist between women – and to which autobiography has contributed in abundant and intricate ways – create a space, which if not yet, will have been.

Notes

1. *Diacritics* 12 (1982) 2–16.
2. See Catherine Belsey, *Critical Practice* (London and New York, Methuen, 1980) pp. 7–14 for a discussion of this term.
3. 'Autobiography in the Aftermath of Romanticism', p. 11.
4. 'Preface', Estelle C. Jelinek ed. *Women's Autobiography: Essays in Criticism* (Bloomington, Indiana University Press, 1980), p. xii.
5. Domna Stanton explains this point in the following way: 'Because of women's different status in the symbolic order, autogynography, I concluded, dramatized the fundamental alterity and non-presence of the subject, even as it asserts itself discursively and strives toward an always impossible self-possession.' 'Autogynography: Is the Subject Different', Domna Stanton ed. *The Female Autograph* (New York, New York Literary Forum, 1984), 5–22, p. 16.
6. See especially: Shari Benstock ed. *The Private Self* (London, Routledge, 1988); Bella Brodski and Celeste Schenk eds. *Life/Lines: Theorizing Women's Autobiography* (Ithaca and London, Cornell University Press, 1988); Leigh Gilmore, *Autobiographics: A Feminist Theory of Women's Self-Representation* (Ithaca and London, Cornell University Press, 1994); Sidonie Smith, *A Poetics of Women's Autobiography* (Bloomington and Indianapolis, Indiana University Press, 1987) and *Subjectivity, Identity and the Body: Women's Autobiographical Practices in the Twentieth Century* (Bloomington and Indianapolis, Indiana University Press, 1993); Sidonie Smith and Julia Watson eds *De/Colonizing the Subject: The Politics of Gender in Women's Autobiography* (Minneapolis, University of Minnesota Press, 1992); Liz Stanley, *The Auto/Biographical I* (Manchester, Manchester University Press, 1992).

7. Leigh Gilmore makes this point and uses the word 'homelier' in *Autobiographics*, p. 2.
8. See Felicity Nusbaum, *The Autobiographical Subject: Gender and Ideology in Eighteenth-Century England* (Baltimore and London, Johns Hopkins University Press, 1989), pp. 30–57 for a historical account of the rise of the unified subject.
9. Christa Wolf, *The Quest for Christa T.* (London, Virago, 1982), p. 170.
10. *Life/Lines*, p. 14.
11. 'Changing the Subject: Authorship, Writing, and the Reader' in *Subject to Change: Reading Feminist Writing* (New York, Columbia University Press, 1988), p. 106.
12. *Speculum of the Other Woman* trans Gillian C. Gill (Ithaca, Cornell University Press, 1985), p. 133.
13. *Of Lies, Secrets and Silence* (London, Virago, 1980), p. 38.
14. This phrase is also the title of a book by Nancy Miller which I discuss below.
15. 'New Combinations: Learning from Virginia Woolf' in Carol Ascher, Louise DeSalvo, Sarah Ruddick eds *Between Women* (Boston, Beacon Press, 1984), p. 137.
16. Introduction, p. xxiii.
17. Preface to *Reading Woman: Essays in Feminist Criticism* (New York, Columbia University Press, 1986), p. x.
18. Rita Felski discusses this autobiographical moment in fiction rather than criticism in *Beyond Feminist Aesthetics* (London, Hutchinson Radius, 1989), pp. 94–6.
19. *Getting Personal* (London and New York, Routledge, 1991), p. 14.
20. Ibid., p.1.
21. See Laura Marcus, 'Personal Criticism and the Autobiographical Turn' in Sally Ledger, Josephine McDonagh and Jane Spencer eds *Political Gender: Texts and Contexts* (Hemel Hempstead, Harvester Wheatsheaf, 1994), pp. 11–27, for a more extended critique of personal criticism.
22. *What Does A Woman Want: Reading and Sexual Difference* (Baltimore and London, Johns Hopkins University Press, 1993), p. 134.
23. *Between Women, What Does a Woman Want*, p. 14.
24. Christa Wolf also expresses this idea in the phrase 'remembered future' which I have incorporated into the title of this book. See 'The Reader and the Writer' in *The Reader and the Writer* (Berlin, Seven Seas Books, 1977), p. 76.
25. *The Quest for Christa T.*, p. 174.
26. For a more extended discussion of the relation between subjectivity and history see my 'The Re-Imagining of History in Contemporary Women's Fiction' in Linda Anderson ed. *Plotting Change: Contemporary Women's Fiction* (London, Edward Arnold, 1990), pp. 129–41.

27. *The Diary of Alice James* ed. Leon Edel (Harmondsworth, Penguin, 1982) p. 34.
28. 'Preliminary Communication' in Sigmund Freud and Joseph Breuer, *Studies on Hysteria*, The Pelican Freud Library (1974), 3, p. 58.
29. *Sexual Subversions* (Sydney, Allen and Unwin, 1989), p. 134.
30. See Margaret Whitford's discussion of Irigaray's view of women's symbolic homelessness in *Luce Irigaray: Philosophy in the Feminine* (London, Routledge, 1991), pp. 156–9.
31. '"The Third Stroke": Reading Woolf with Freud' in Susan Sheridan ed. *Grafts* (London, Verso, 1988), pp. 93–110 (p. 94). Susannah Radstone also discusses this essay and feminist nostalgia in 'Remembering Medea: The Uses of Nostalgia', *Critical Quarterly* 35 (1993), 54–63.
32. 'Reading Woolf with Freud', p. 105.
33. Ibid., p. 105.
34. Ibid., p. 109.
35. *Sexes and Genealogies* trans Gillian C. Gill (New York, Columbia University Press, 1993), pp. 153–65 (p. 155).
36. Ibid., p. 164.
37. Ibid., p. 155.

Chapter 2

I cite various letters by Alice James. Where possible I refer to the published texts in Ruth Bernard Yeazell ed. *The Death and Letters of Alice James* (Berkeley, University of California Press, 1981). Letters not included in her selection are in the James papers, Houghton Library, Harvard University. Alice's letters to Annie Ashburner are in The National Library of Scotland.

1. *The Diary of Alice James*, ed. Leon Edel (Harmondsworth, Penguin, 1982), p. 31. All further references to the Diary are included in the text.
2. Alice had two other brothers, Garth Wilkinson and Robertson, neither of whom wrote, and who as a consequence felt profoundly alienated from the family in later life.
3. See Jean Strouse, *Alice James: A Biography* (London, Bantam Books, 1980), p. 353.
4. 'Emphasis Added: Plots and Plausibilities in Women's Fiction' in *Subject to Change* (New York, Columbia University Press, 1988), p. 43.
5. See Jean Strouse, pp. ix–x.
6. To William James, 10 September 1886 (Houghton Library, 1476)
7. Diary, p. 104

8. To Alice and William James, 21 August 1888, in Yeazell, p. 145.
9. To William James, 22 March 1889, in Yeazell, p. 162.
10. Diary, p. 185.
11. For an interesting linking of women's autobiography with 'monstrosity' see Barbara Johnson, 'My Monster/My Self', *Diacritics* 12 (1982), 2–10.
12. 'Freud's Masterplot: Questions of Narrative', *Yale French Studies* 55/56 (1977), 280–300 (pp. 282–4).
13. Preface to *Roderick Hudson* in *The Art of the Novel* with an introduction by Richard P. Blackmur (London, Charles Scribner, 1935), p. 6.
14. See Walter Benjamin, 'The Storyteller' in *Illuminations* (London, Fontana, 1973), p. 94.
15. 'Notes of a Son and Brother' in *Henry James: Autobiography* (London, W.H. Allen, 1956), p. 411
16. I was alerted to this phrase, which comes from the Preface to the New York edition of *The Tragic Muse*, by Adeline R. Tintner's article, 'Autobiography as Fiction: "The Usurping Consciousness" as Hero of James's Memoirs', *Twentieth Century Literature* 23 (1977), 239–59
17. For an account of Woman as art 'object' see Susan Gubar, '"The Blank Page" and the Issues of Female Creativity' in *Writing and Sexual Difference* ed. Elizabeth Abel (Hemel Hempstead, Harvester Wheatsheaf, 1982), pp. 73–93.
18. Letter to H.G. Wells, 10 July, 1915 in *Henry James and H.G. Wells* ed. with introduction by Leon Edel and Gordon N. Ray (London, Rupert Hart-Davis, 1958), p. 267.
19. *Critical Practice* (London, Methuen, 1980), p. 65.
20. Strouse, p. xvi.
21. 'Notes of a Son and Brother', p. 268.
22. Ibid. p. 301.
23. 'Convert' is a term frequently used by Henry James. See 'Notes of a Son and Brother', p. 280.
24. To William James, 30 July 1891, in Yeazell, p. 187.
25. William James, 'Some Problems of Philosophy: A Beginning of an Introduction to Philosophy' (1911) quoted in Richard A. Hocks, *Henry James and Pragmatic Thought* (Berkeley, University of California Press, 1974), p. 88.
26. To Frances Morse, 11 April 1886? (Houghton 1510).
27. 'The Art of Fiction' in *The House of Fiction: Essays on the Novel by Henry James* ed. Leon Edel (London, Rupert Hart-Davis, 1957), p. 33
28. 'The Art of Fiction', p. 32.
29. 'Notes of a Son and Brother', p. 279.
30. Preface to *Portrait of a Lady* in *The Art of the Novel*, p. 48.
31. 'Woman and the Literary Text' in *The Rights and Wrongs of Woman*

ed. Anne Oakley and Juliet Mitchell (Harmondsworth, Penguin, 1976), pp. 228, 230.

32. Preface to *Portrait of a Lady*, p. 50.

33. See Diana Collecott, 'Framing the *Portrait of a Lady*', *Writing Women* 1 (1981), 66–79; revised version in Amritjit Singh and Ayyapa Paniker eds *The Magic Circle of Henry James* (New York, Envoy Press 1988).

34. To Annie Ashburner, 12 April 1876, in Yeazell, pp. 72–3.

35. Quoted in Strouse, p. 47.

36. 'Notes of a Son and Brother', p. 343.

37. Strouse, p. 28.

38. For an alternative point of view on spinsterhood in this period see Sheila Jeffreys, *The Spinster and her Enemies* (London, Pandora, 1985), pp. 86–101.

39. To Annie Ashburner, 12 April 1876, in Yeazell, p. 74.

40. To Annie Ashburner, 28 December 1876 (National Library).

41. To Annie Ashburner, 19 October, 1877? (National Library).

42. To Sara Darwin, 23 September 1876 (Houghton 1433).

43. To William James, 3–7 January 1886?, in Yeazell, p. 107.

44. To Annie Ashburner, 12 April 1876, in Yeazell, p. 74.

45. See Carroll Smith-Rosenberg, 'Puberty to Menopause: The Cycle of Femininity in Nineteenth-Century America' in *Disorderly Conduct* (Oxford, Oxford University Press, 1985), pp. 182–196.

46. See Julia Kristeva, 'Women's Time', in *The Kristeva Reader* ed. Toril Moi (Oxford, Basil Blackwell, 1986), pp. 187–213 (p. 192).

47. To William James, 25 May 1894, in Henry James, *Letters* 3 vols (London, Macmillan, 1974) ed. Leon Edel, III, p. 481.

48. 'The Hysterical Woman: Sex Roles and Role Conflict in Nineteenth-Century America' in *Disorderly Conduct*, p. 207.

49. See Jacqueline Rose, 'Jeffrey Masson and Alice James', *Oxford Literary Review* 8 (1986), 185–92.

50. 'Case 5: Fraulein Elizabeth Von R' in Sigmund Freud and Joseph Breuer, *Studies on Hysteria*, The Pelican Freud Library (1974) 3, p. 231.

51. 'Preliminary Communication' in *Studies on Hysteria*, p. 58.

52. See Mary Jacobus's very important discussion of hysteria and women's writing, to which I am indebted, in *Reading Woman: Essays in Feminist Criticism* (New York, Columbia University Press, 1986), pp. 197–274.

53. 'The Psychotherapy of Hysteria' in *Studies on Hysteria*, p. 380.

54. Diary, pp. 222–3.

55. Jacobus, pp. 211–12.

56. To William James, 3–7 January 1886, in Yeazell, pp. 106–7.

57. To Catherine Walsh, 31 January 1885, in Yeazell, pp. 101–2.

58. Diary, p. 142.

59. Howard Feinstein, *Becoming William James* (Ithaca, Cornell University Press, 1984), p. 201.
60. *The Varieties of Religious Experience* (Harmondsworth, Penguin, 1982), pp. 161–2.
61. *Essays in Psychology* (Cambridge, Harvard University Press, 1983), p. 264.
62. *In Dora's Case* ed. Charles Bernheimer and Claire Kahane (London, Virago, 1985), p. 21.
63. 'Femininity, Narrative and Psychoanalysis' in *Women: The Longest Revolution* (London, Virago, 1984), p. 290.
64. *Reading Woman*, pp. 215–16.
65. Letter to Catherine Walsh, 31 January 1885, in Yeazell, p.103: 'I am sorry to send so dull a letter but I have no annals but those of a sick room.'
66. 'The New Model Autobiographer', *New Literary History* 9 (1977–8), 51–63 (p. 56)
67. 'The New Model Autobiographer', p. 55.
68. (Bloomington, Indiana University Press, 1985), p. 15.
69. This phrase is Nancy Miller's and forms the title of her book, *The Heroine's Text: Readings in the French and English Novel, 1722–1782* (New York, Columbia University Press, 1981).
70. 'The New Model Autobiographer', p. 55.
71. The most famous formulation of this problem is Emile Beneveniste's; see 'Subjectivity in Language' in *Problems in General Linguistics* (Florida: University of Miami Press, 1971), pp. 223–30.
72. Sturrock uses the example of Michael Leiris's *La regle du jeu* (Paris, Gallimard, 1948–76) but Roland Barthes' *Roland Barthes par Roland Barthes* (Paris, Editions du Seuil, 1975) trans. Richard Howard (London, Macmillan, 1977) could also be cited here.
73. *This Sex Which Is Not One* trans. Catherine Porter with Carolyn Burke (Ithaca, Cornell University Press, 1985), p. 76.
74. *Speculum of the Other Woman* trans. Gillian C. Gill (Ithaca, Cornell University Press, 1985), pp. 71–2. See also Margaret Whitford, *Luce Irigaray: Philosophy in the Feminine* (London, Routledge, 1991), p. 71.
75. *Jacques Lacan: A Feminist Introduction* (London, Routledge 1990), p. 174.
76. We could compare this term of self-deprecation with Nathaniel Hawthorne's famous dismissal in 1855 of the 'd. . .d mob of scribbling women' who were in his eyes taking over the literary market.
77. *Camera Lucida* (London, Fontana, 1984), p. 65
78. Quoted in Julia Kristeva, 'Women's Time', p. 191.
79. *Camera Lucida*, p. 65.
80. 'About Chinese Women' in *The Kristeva Reader*, p. 150.

81. See Strouse, p. 329.
82. For a very interesting discussion of James's secrecy and its connection to sexuality see Eve Kokofsky Sedgewick, 'The Beast in the Closet' in *The Epistemology of the Closet* (Hemel Hempstead, Harvester Wheatsheaf, 1991), pp. 196–7.
83. Michel Foucault, 'What is An Author' in Josue Harari ed. *Textual Strategies: Perspectives in Post-Structuralist Criticism* (Ithaca, Cornell University Press, 1979).
84. I'm thinking of the last paragraph of 'Castration or Decapitation', *Signs*, 7 (1981), 41–55 (p. 55): 'Culturally speaking, women have wept a great deal, but once the tears are shed, there will be endless laughter instead. Laughter that breaks out, overflows, a humor no one would expect to find in women – which is nonetheless surely their greatest strength because it's a humor that sees man much further away than he has ever been seen.'

Chapter 3

1. *A Room of One's Own* (London, Hogarth Press, 1929; London, Granada, 1977), p. 6. All further references are to the Granada edition and are included in the text.
2. The four Marys that Woolf refers to come from a well-known Scottish Ballad:

> Last night there were four Marys
> Tonight there'll be but three
> There was Mary Beton, and Mary Seton
> And Mary Carmichael and me.

As Shoshana Felman has pointed out Woolf's text thus addresses us in the voice of a woman who is 'voiceless, executed, dead'. See *What Does A Woman Want: Reading and Sexual Difference* (Baltimore and London, Johns Hopkins University Press, 1993), pp. 142–5.
3. 'Penelope at Work: Interruptions in *A Room of One's Own*', *Novel*, 1982, 5–18, (p. 8).
4. *Virginia Woolf: Feminist Destinations* (Oxford, Basil Blackwell, 1988), pp. 17–18.
5. *Feminism Without Women: Culture and Criticism in a 'Postfeminist' Age* (London and New York, Routledge, 1991), pp. 55–6.
6. Woolf's 'flights of words' winging their way 'illegitimately' into existence strangely anticipate Hélène Cixous' punning use of 'voler' as meaning both flight and theft. 'To fly/steal is woman's gesture, to steal into language to make it fly.' See Hélène Cixous and Catherine Clément, *The Newly Born Woman* 1975; trans. Betsy Wing (Minneapolis, University of Minnesota Press, 1986), p. 96.

7. I am indebted to Peggy Kamuf's subtle analysis of this passage whilst finding her encounter with Foucault and the deflection away from issues to do with gender more problematic. See 'Penelope at Work: Interruptions in *A Room of One's Own*', p. 17.

8. 'It follows that a feminist practice can only be negative, at odds with what already exists so that we may say "that's not it" and "that's still not it." In "woman" I see something that cannot be represented, something that is not said, something above and beyond nomenclatures and ideologies.' Julia Kristeva, 'Woman Can Never Be Defined', *Tel Quel*, 1974; extract published in *New French Feminisms* ed. Elaine Marks and Isabelle de Courtivron (Hemel Hempstead, Harvester Wheatsheaf), 1981, pp. 136–41.

9. See Shoshana Felman, *What Does A Woman Want*, pp. 139–142.

10. For discussion of Woolf's work in light of contemporary theory see particularly Makiko Minow-Pinkney, *Virginia Woolf and the Problem of the Subject* (Hemel Hempstead, Harvester Wheatsheaf, 1987) and Rachel Bowlby, *Virginia Woolf: Feminist Destinations*.

11. Smyth's publications included: *Impressions that Remained* 2 vols (London, Longmans, 1919); *Streaks of Life* (London, Longmans, 1921); *A Three-Legged Tour in Greece* (London, Heinemann, 1927); *A Final Burning of Boats Etc.* (London, Longmans, 1928); *Female Pipings in Eden* (London, Peter Davies, 1933); *Beecham and Pharaoh* (London, Chapman and Hall, 1935); *As Time Went On* (London, Longmans, 1936). The book which is under discussion here, Smyth's last autobiographical volume, is *What Happened Next* (London, Longmans, 1940). For a discussion of Smyth's relationship with Woolf see Suzanne Raitt, '"The Tide of Ethel": Femininity as Narrative in the Friendship of Ethel Smyth and Virginia Woolf', *Critical Quarterly* 30 (1988), 3–21.

12. *The Letters* ed. Nigel Nicolson, 6 vols (London, The Hogarth Press, 1980), VI, p. 453 (24 Dec. 1940). Further references to *The Letters* are included in the text.

13. *Collected Essays*, 4 vols (London, The Hogarth Press, 1967), II, p. 286. All further references to the essays are to this edition and will be included in the text.

14. 'The Difference of View' in *Reading Woman* (New York, Columbia University Press, 1986), pp. 39–40.

15. *The Diary of Virginia Woolf* ed. Anne Oliver Bell, 5 vols (The Hogarth Press, 1982; Harmondsworth, Penguin 1983), III, p. 203. This and all further references are to the Penguin edition and are included in the text.

16. Trans Geoffrey Bennington and Rachel Bowlby (London, Routledge, 1990), p. 6.

17. See Daniel Ferrer, *Virginia Woolf and the Madness of Language*, p. 6.

18. *Writing and Gender: Virginia Woolf's Writing Practice* (Hemel Hempstead, Harvester Wheatsheaf, 1990), p. 5.

19. The idea of 'screening' is discussed extensively by Sue Roe. See *Writing and Gender*, particularly pp. 21–2; 58–9.

20. 'These are traveller's notes which I offer myself shd I again be lost.' *Diary*, V, p. 250 (26 January 1940).

21. 'The public world very notably invaded the private at MH. last weekend.' *Diary*, V, p. 131 (22 March 1938).

22. *A Passionate Apprenticeship: The Early Journals 1897–1909* ed. Mitchell A. Leaska (London, The Hogarth Press, 1990), p. 393.

23. *A Passionate Apprenticeship*, pp. 281–2 (11 August 1905).

24. 'A Sketch of the Past' in *Moments of Being* ed. Jeanne Schulkind (London, Granada, 1978), pp. 86–7.

25. *Virginia Woolf: A Writer's Life* (Oxford, Oxford University Press, 1984), p. 173.

26. 'Beyond Determinism: George Eliot and Virginia Woolf' in *Women Writing and Writing About Women* ed. Mary Jacobus (Croom Helm, London, 1979), p. 95.

27. 'What a mercy to have this page to uncramp in!' *Diary*, V, p. 80 (21 April 1937).

28. Woolf complained in her diary about writing her biography of Roger Fry: 'its all too detailed, too tied down – I must expand, first on this irresponsible page, & then, for four days I swear, before we go back on Sunday, in fiction.' *Diary*, V, p. 197 (9 January 1939).

29. 'Deliberation' in *A Barthes Reader* ed. Susan Sontag (London, Jonathan Cape, 1982), pp. 494–5.

30. 'The Death of the Author' (1968) reprinted in Philip Rice and Patricia Waugh eds *Modern Literary Theory: A Reader* (London, Edward Arnold, 1989), pp. 114–17 (p. 117).

31. 'Playing: The Search for the Self' in *Playing and Reality* (Harmondsworth, Penguin, 1980), p. 75.

32. 'If one could be friendly with women, what a pleasure – the relationship so secret & private compared with relations with men. Why not write about it? truthfully? As I think, this diary writing has greatly helped my style; loosened the ligatures.' (*D*, II, p. 320).

33. (Los Angeles, J.P. Tarcher, 1958), p. 57.

34. Ibid., p. 144.

35. See Julia Kristeva: 'The imaginary of the work of art, that is really the most extraordinary and the most unsettling imitation of the mother–child dependence.' From an interview in *Cahiers du GRIF*, 32, quoted in Toril Moi ed. *The Kristeva Reader* (Oxford, Blackwell, 1986), p. 14.

36. The passage from the diary cited above continues: 'I have cut the string that ties me to that quivering bag of nerves – all its gratifications and acute despairs.'

37. Luce Irigaray, 'Volume Without Contours' in Margaret Whitford ed. *The Irigaray Reader* (Oxford, Blackwell, 1991), p. 55.
38. For a description of Woolf's 'looking-glass shame' see 'A Sketch of the Past', pp. 79–80. She recorded her anxiety about photographs in her diary: 'I feel that my privacy is invaded; my legs show; & I am revealed to the world (1,000 at most) as a plain dowdy old woman' (*D*, IV, p. 124).
39. 'Volume without Contours', p. 55.
40. 'Often now I have to control my excitement – as if I were pushing through a screen . . . What this portends I don't know . . . Often it is connected with the sea & St Ives.' (*D*, II, P. 246)
41. See Jeanne Schulkind's 'Editor's Note' to *Moments of Being*.
42. See 'Modern Fiction', *Collected Essays*, II, p. 104.
43. Alan Bell ed. *Sir Leslie Stephen's Mausoleum Book* (Oxford, Clarendon, 1977). All references to this book are hereafter included in the text.
44. Letter of 28 June 1895, quoted in Alan Bell's Introduction to the *Mausoleum Book*, p. x.
45. 'Virginia Woolf's *Moments of Being* and Autobiographical Tradition in the Stephen Family', *Journal of Modern Literature* 10 (1983), 175–96.
46. 'Reflections in the Looking-Glass: Leslie Stephen and Virginia Woolf', *Journal of Modern Literature* 10 (1983), 197–216 (p. 209).
47. *A Room of One's Own*, pp. 72–3.
48. *Woman of Letters* (London, Pandora, 1978), p. 17.
49. *The Hands of the Living God* (London, The Hogarth Press, 1969), p. 122.
50. 'Revolution in Poetic Language', in *The Kristeva Reader*, pp. 93–4.
51. 'Revolution in Poetic Language', p. 93; Kristeva mentions Winnicott in 'A Question of Subjectivity – An Interview', *Women's Review* 12; reprinted in *Modern Literary Theory: A Reader*, pp. 130–1.
52. *The Hands of the Living God*, p. 122.
53. Ibid., p. 53.
54. See Elizabeth Grosz, *Jacques Lacan: A Feminist Introduction* (London, Routledge, 1990), pp. 38–9.
55. See 'Motherhood According to Giovanni Bellini' in *Desire in Language* (Oxford, Basil Blackwell, 1980), pp. 239–41.
56. *Sexual Subversions: Three French Feminists* (Sydney, Allen and Unwin, 1989), p. 72.
57. *Powers of Horror: An Essay on Abjection* trans Leon S. Roudiez (New York, Columbia University Press 1982), p. 2.
58. Ibid., p. 12.
59. The phrase 'benign circle' is Melanie Klein's. See 'Love, Guilt and Reparation' in *Love, Guilt and Reparation & Other Works 1921–1945* (London, The Hogarth Press, 1975), p. 340.

60. Hermione Lee discusses this passage extensively in her essay 'A Burning Glass: Reflection in Virginia Woolf' in Eric Warner ed. *Virginia Woolf: A Centenary Perspective* (London, Macmillan, 1984). I am grateful to her for pointing out the significance of this passage to me though I want to draw different conclusions from it.
61. See Sidonie Smith, *Subjectivity, Identity and the Body* (Bloomington and Indianapolis, Indiana University Press, 1993), p. 94 for a discussion of this passage.
62. *Writing and Gender*, p. 43.
63. *Virginia Woolf and the Madness of Language*, p. 8.
64. *Speculum of the Other Woman*, trans. Gillian C. Gill (Ithaca, Cornell University Press, 1985), p. 146.
65. *Speculum of the Other Woman*, p. 146.

Chapter 4

1. 'Modern Fiction', *Collected Essays*, 4 vols (London, The Hogarth Press, 1967) 2, p. 286.
2. 'Caterpillars of the World Unite', *Scrutiny* (September, 1938), pp. 210–11.
3. *A Literature of Their Own* (London, Virago, 1978), p. 285.
4. First published Victor Gollancz 1933; this and all future references are to the Virago edition, published 1978.
5. For a very full and provocative discussion of the thinking about and treatment of trauma in the period of the First World War see Ruth Leys, 'Traumatic Cures: Shell Shock, and the Question of Memory', *Critical Inquiry* 20 (1994), 623–62.
6. 'Moses and Monotheism', The Penguin Freud Library, vol. 13, p. 310.
7. 'Introduction', *American Imago* 48 no. 1 (1991), 1–12 (p. 7).
8. 'History and Ideology in Autobiographical Literature of the First World War', *Mosaic* 23 (1990), 37–54 (p. 41).
9. *Undertones of War* (New York, Harcourt, Brace & World, 1965; first published 1928), pp. 11–12.
10. *Memoirs of an Infantry Officer* (London, Faber, 1965; first published 1930), p. 93; p.183.
11. 'Introduction', *American Imago* 48 no. 4 (1991), 417–24 (p. 420).
12. See Evelyn Cobley, 'History and Ideology in Autobiographical Literature', pp. 44–5.
13. See Sharon Ouditt, *Fighting Forces, Writing Women* (London, Routledge, 1993), pp. 169–75.
14. 'History and Ideology', p. 42.
15. *Subjectivities: A History of Self-Representation in Britain, 1832–1920* (Oxford, Oxford University Press, 1991), p. 4.

16. *Testament of Experience*, first published Victor Gollancz, 1957; this and all future references are to the Virago edition, 1979.
17. *The Dark Tide*, 1923; *Not Without Honour*, 1924; *Women's Work in Modern England*, 1928; *Halcyon, or, The Future of Monogamy*, 1929. Marvin Rintala offers a very negative assessment of Brittain as writer, arguing 'Brittain's literary reputation therefore rests entirely upon her non-fiction, especially her explicitly autobiographical works.' See 'Chronicler of a Generation: Vera Brittain's Testament', *Journal of Political and Military Sociology*, 12 (1984), 23–35 (p. 24).
18. See Martin Pugh, *Women and the Women's Movement in Britain 1914–1959* (London, Macmillan, 1992), pp. 90–100.
19. *Back to Home and Duty: Women Between the Wars 1918–1939* (London, Pandora, 1989), pp. 56–60.
20. See *Testament of Experience*, p. 45.
21. Vera Brittain wrote in her Diary: 'Oh that University Woman's Club – full of grim looking desiccated spinsters in appalling tweeds. Heaven preserve Shirley from an academic career.' Alan Bishop ed. *Chronicle of a Friendship: Vera Brittain's Diary of the Thirties, 1932–1939* (London, Gollancz, 1986), p. 339. Quoted in Deirdre Beddoe, *Back to Home and Duty*, p. 27.
22. 'Conditions and Limits of Autobiography' in James Olney ed. *Autobiography: Essays Theoretical and Critical* (Princeton, Princeton University Press, 1980), p. 39.
23. Nancy Miller, 'Writing Fictions: Women's Autobiography in France' in *Subject to Change* (New York, Columbia University Press, 1988), p. 52.
24. See Johanna Alberti, *Beyond Suffrage: Feminists in War and Peace 1914–28* (London, Macmillan, 1989), p. 12.
25. Allan Bishop ed. *Chronicle of a Friendship*, p. 201.
26. Preface, *I Have Been Young* (London, Victor Gollancz, 1935).
27. In discussion at History Workshop Conference 21, Newcastle 1987. See also her *Beyond Suffrage*, p. 4.
28. In Bella Brodski and Celeste Schenck eds *Life/Lines* (Ithaca and London, Cornell University Press, 1988), p. 41.
29. Ibid., p. 22.
30. In Shari Benstock ed. *The Private Self: Theory and Practice of Women's Autobiographical Writings* (London, Routledge, 1988), p. 34.
31. Ibid., p. 44.
32. 'Making the Most of Martyrdom: Harriet Martineau, Autobiography and Death', *Literature and History* 2 (1993), 24–45 (p. 26).
33. See Joan W. Scott, 'Deconstructing Equality-Versus-Difference' in Marianne Hirsch and Evelyn Fox Keller eds *Conflicts in Feminism* (London and New York, Routledge, 1990), pp. 138–9.

34. 'Reading Double: Sand's Difference' in Nancy K. Miller ed. *The Poetics of Gender*, New York, Columbia University Press, 1986, p. 267.
35. See Diana Fuss's argument about the inside/outside model and how it signifies in the construction of identity, in her introduction to *Inside/ Out: Lesbian Theories, Gay Theories* ed. Diana Fuss (New York, Routledge, 1991).
36. (Oxford, Oxford University Press, 1975), p. 30.
37. Ibid., p. 35.
38. *Blindness and Insight* (London, Methuen, 1993), p. 212
39. Ibid., p. 216.
40. Ibid., p. 222.
41. *No Man's Land: Combat and Identity in World War 1* (Cambridge, Cambridge University Press, 1979), p. 3.
42. Ibid., p. 38.
43. In Margaret Randoph Higonnet *et al.* eds *Behind the Lines: Gender and the Two World Wars* (New Haven and London, Yale University Press, 1987), p. 223.
44. This is a quotation from Leed, p. 163.
45. See Jacqueline Rose's fascinating argument about war and knowledge in her essay 'Why War?' published in *Why War?*, (Oxford, Blackwell, 1994).
46. In *Behind the Lines: Gender and the Two World Wars*, p. 35.
47. '"It seems to me that the War will make a big division of 'before' and 'after' in the history of the world, almost if not quite as big as the 'B.C.' and 'A.D.' division made by the birth of Christ."' *Testament of Youth* (London, Victor Gollancz, 1933; London, Virago, 1978), p. 317.
48. 'Fetishism and its Ironies', in *Bad Objects: Essays Popular and Unpopular* (Durham and London, Duke University Press, 1995), p. 105.
49. 'Mourning and Melancholia' in The Pelican Freud Library, 11, 1974. pp. 251–68.
50. Ibid., p. 268.
51. *Black Sun: Depression and Melancholia* (New York, Columbia University Press, 1989), p. 10.
52. Ibid., p. 43.
53. Ibid., p. 53.
54. Ibid., p. 40.
55. Ibid., p. 103
56. Ibid., p. 48.
57. Ibid., p. 60.
58. Ibid., p. 104.

Chapter 5

1. *The Journals of Sylvia Plath* ed. Frances McCullough with Ted Hughes (New York, Ballantine Books, 1982) p. 24. I discuss this quotation fully on pages 103–4.

2. Ted Hughes tells us in his Foreword to the published journals: 'The journals exist in an assortment of notebooks and bunches of loose sheets. This selection contains about a third of the whole bulk, which is now in The Neilson Library at Smith College' (p. xv).

3. See Saul Maloff: 'Only the names were changed, nothing else: as much as a novel can be, it was recorded rather than imagined' in 'Waiting for the Voice to Crack', *New Republic*, 8 May 1971, reprinted in Linda W. Wagner ed. *Sylvia Plath: The Critical Heritage* (London and New York, Routledge, 1988) p. 103.

4. Introduction, *Sylvia Plath: The Critical Heritage*, p. 1.

5. Typical examples of 'hysterical' criticism are: Stephen Spender: 'They are nothing more than poems of prophecy, written by some priestess, cultivating her hysteria' in 'Warnings from the Grave', *New Republic*, 18 June 1966, reprinted in *Sylvia Plath: The Critical Heritage*, pp. 69–73 (p. 72); or P.N. Furbank: 'It is no good pretending that Sylvia Plath's is not sick verse . . . the art for all its power, is an hysterical bravado in the face of insuperable calamity' in 'New Poetry', *Listener*, 11 March 1965, also reprinted in *Sylvia Plath: The Critical Heritage*, pp. 73–4.

6. Jacqueline Rose, *The Haunting of Sylvia Plath* (London, Virago, 1991), see pp. 4–8.

7. See Neil Hertz, 'Medusa's Head: Male Hysteria Under Political Pressure' in *The End of the Line* (New York, Columbia University Press, 1985), pp. 161–93.

8. *The Haunting of Sylvia Plath*, p. 17.

9. Ricocheting was the word Plath used to describe her movement between different states of mind: 'I could go mad ricocheting in between.' See *The Journals*, p. 24.

10. *No Respect: Intellectuals and Popular Culture* (London, Routledge, 1989), p. 16.

11. (Faber, London, 1963). All further references to *The Bell Jar* are to this edition and are included in the text.

12. *No Respect*, p. 20.

13. See *The Journals*, p. 25.

14. For a discussion of the uses of Freud and psychoanalysis in the period see Janet Walker, 'Hollywood, Freud and the Representation of Women' in *Home is Where the Heart Is* ed. Christine Gledhill (London, British Film Institute, 1987), pp. 197–214.

15. This phrase is Tania Modleski's and forms part of the title of her book *Loving with a Vengeance: Mass-Produced Fantasies for Women* (London, Methuen, 1982).
16. *For Her Own Good* (London, Pluto Press, 1979), p. 255.
17. *Letters Home* (London, Faber, 1976), p. 473 (21 October, 1962).
18. Ibid., p. 433 (22 October 1961).
19. For a discussion of the *Ladies Home Journal* and Plath's relationship to it see Rose, pp. 175–9.
20. Alison Light, '"Returning to Manderley" – Romance Fiction, Female Sexuality and Class', *Feminist Review* 16 (1984), reprinted in Mary Eagleton ed. *Feminist Literary Theory* (Oxford, Blackwell, 1986), p. 140.
21. Jean Radford, Introduction in *The Progress of Romance: The Politics of Popular Fiction* (London, Routledge and Kegan Paul, 1986), p. 12.
22. *Loving With A Vengeance*, p. 41.
23. *Female Desire: Women's Sexuality Today* (London, Paladin, 1984), p. 195.
24. *Feminism Without Women: Culture and Criticism in a 'Postfeminist' Age* (London and New York, Routledge, 1991), p. 43.
25. Ibid., p. 45.
26. See Rita Felski, *Beyond Feminist Aesthetics* (London, Hutchinson Radius, 1989), pp. 86–121 for an interesting discussion of the problems of 'Confession' and in particular feminist confessional writing.
27. See Chapter 3, pp. 68–9.
28. *Modern Language Notes* 94 (1979), pp. 919–30.
29. See Neil Hertz, 'Afterword; The End of the Line' in *The End of the Line* (New York, Columbia University Press, 1985) and 'Lurid Figures' in Lindsay Waters and Wlad Godzich eds *Reading de Man Reading* (Minneapolis, University of Minnesota Press, 1989).
30. Neil Hertz, 'Afterword: The End of the Line', p. 223.
31. Teresa de Lauretis, 'The Violence of Rhetoric' in *Technologies of Gender* (London, Macmillan, 1987).
32. 'The Violence of Rhetoric', pp. 41–2.
33. See Tania Modleski for pertinent comments about the gendering of the body and how women are made to bear 'the burdens of masculine ambivalence about the body' in *Feminism Without Men*, pp. 109–11.
34. Quoted in Lois Ames 'A Biographical Note', *The Bell Jar* (New York, Faber, 1971), p. 294.
35. See *The Haunting of Sylvia Plath*, p. 185.
36. 'The Autobiographical Contract' in Tzevtan Todorov ed. *French Literary Theory Today: A Reader* (Cambridge, Cambridge University Press, 1982).
37. See Rita Felski, *Beyond Feminist Aesthetics*, p. 91.
38. 'Writing Fictions: Women's Autobiography in France' in *Subject to*

Change: Reading Feminist Writing (New York, Columbia University Press, 1988).

39. *The Haunting of Sylvia Plath*, p. 184.

40. 'Extreme Fidelity' in Susan Sellers ed. *Writing Differences: Reading from the Seminars of Hélène Cixous* (Milton Keynes, Open University Press, 1988) p. 34.

41. See Maud Ellmann, *The Hunger Artists: Starving, Writing and Imprisonment* (Cambridge, Harvard University Press, 1993) for an interesting account of the relation between eating, the Other and writing which fed my own thinking here.

42. 'Fear of Breakdown', *International Review of Psychoanalysis*, 1 (1974), p. 176.

43. See Anne Stevenson 'Writing as a Woman' in *Women Writing and Writing About Women* ed. Mary Jacobus (London, Croom Helm, 1979), p. 162.

44. It is worth thinking about this point in relation to readings of *The Bell Jar* which see the Rosenberg's execution as symbolically prefiguring Esther's later electric shock treatment.

Chapter 6

1. 'An Interview: Audre Lorde and Adrienne Rich' in *Sister Outsider* (New York, Crossing Press, 1984). All references to this essay are included in the text.

2. (London, Macmillan, 1982).

3. 'Do not swallow yourself up, do not swallow me down in that which flows from you to me. I'd like it so much if we could be there, both of us. So that one does not disappear into the other, or the other into the one.' 'And the One Does not Stir without the Other', *Signs*, 7 (1), 1981, 60–67 (p. 11).

4. Gallop cites a passage from 'L'Herethique de l'amour' where the first person pronoun belongs to the mother: 'What relation between me, or even more modestly my body and this internal fold-graft which, once the umbilical cord cut, is an inaccessible other? My body and . . . it. No relation'. (p. 116).

5. 'Motherhood According to Giovanni Bellini' in *Desire in Language* (Oxford, Basil Blackwell, 1980), p. 235.

6. *Feminism and Psychoanalysis*, p. 116.

7. From 'of Chinese Women'. quoted in Gallop, *Feminism and Psychoanalysis,* p. 121.

8. See Margaret Whitford, 'Reading Irigaray in the Nineties' in Carolyn Burke *et al.* eds *Engaging with Irigaray* (New York, Columbia University Press, 1994), pp. 15–33.

9. 'The Three Genders' in *Sexes and Genealogies* (New York, Columbia University Press, 1993), p. 181.

10. 'The Limits of the Transference' in *The Irigaray Reader* (Oxford, Blackwell, 1991), p. 107.

11. Ibid., p. 108.

12. Ibid., p. 108.

13. Ibid., p. 110.

14. Ibid., p. 108.

15. 'Women, the Sacred and Money' in *Sexes and Genealogies*, p. 86; quoted in Elizabeth Hirsch, 'Back in Analysis: Things to do with Irigaray', in *Engaging with Irigaray*, pp. 285–315.

16. (London, Virago, 1977).

17. The 'New Introduction' is printed without page numbers, presumably so as not to interfere with the pagination of the original edition.

18. 'Does Sex Have a History', *New Formations* 1 (Spring 1987), p. 35, quoted in 'Introduction: Terms of Reference' in Elizabeth Weed ed. *Coming to Terms* (London and New York, Routledge, 1989), p. xix.

19. 'A Manifesto for Cyborgs: Science, Technology, and Socialist Feminism in the 1980s' in Elizabeth Weed ed. *Coming to Terms*, p. 179.

20. In *On Lies, Secrets and Silence* (London, Virago, 1977), pp. 33–49.

21. *Feminism and Geography* (Cambridge, Polity Press, 1993), p. 149.

22. See Rose, *Feminism and Geography*, p. 149 and my discussion of Peggy Kamuf's 'Penelope at Work: Interruptions on *A Room of One's Own*' in Chapter 3, pages 44–6.

23. 'A Man's Place' in Alice Jardine and Paul Smith eds *Men in Feminism* (New York, Methuen, 1987), p. 77, p. 75.

24. 'In a Word: Interview' in *Outside in the Teaching Machine* (London and New York, Routledge, 1993), p. 22.

25. 'Women, Chora, Dwelling' in *Space, Time and Perversion* (London and New York, Routledge, 1995), p. 121.

26. 'Previous Engagements: The Receptions of Irigaray' in Burke *et al.*, *Engaging with Irigaray*, p. 12.

27. Schor is here quoting Margaret Whitford. See *Luce Irigaray: Philosophy in the Feminine* (London, Routledge, 1991), p. 143.

28. 'Architecture from the Outside' in *Space, Time and Perversion*, p. 131.

29. *Blood, Bread and Poetry* (London, Virago, 1987), p. 160. All further page references to essays from this collection are included in the text.

30. 'In a Word: *Interview*', p. 6.

31. 'The Problem of Speaking for Others', *Cultural Critique* 20 (1991–2), 5–32 (p. 16).

32. Ibid., p. 23.

33. Ibid., pp. 20–1.

34. See Donna Harraway, 'A Manifesto for Cyborgs', p. 197 and Linda

Alcoff, 'Cultural Feminism versus Poststructuralism: The Identity Crisis in Feminist Theory', *Signs* 13 (1988), p. 413.

35. See Nancy Miller, 'Changing the Subject: Authorship, Writing and the Reader' in *Subject to Change* (New York, Columbia University Press, 1988), pp. 109–11 and Harriet Davidson, '"I say I am There": Siting/ Citing the Subject of Feminism and Deconstruction' in Cathy Caruth and Deborah Esch eds *Critical Encounters: Reference and Responsibility in Deconstructive Writing* (New Brunswick, New Jersey, Rutgers University Press, 1995), pp. 241–61.

36. 'Introduction: Terms of Reference' in *Coming to Terms*, pp. xv–xvi.

37. *What Does A Woman Want?*(Baltimore and London, Johns Hopkins University Press, 1993), pp. 133–4.

38. *Thinking Through the Body* (New York, Columbia University Press, 1988), pp. 4–5.

39. (New York, Crossing Press). All references are to this edition and contained within the text.

Works cited

Alberti, Johanna, *Beyond Suffrage: Feminists in War and Peace 1914–28* (London, Macmillan, 1989).

Alcoff, Linda, 'Cultural Feminism versus Postructuralism: The Identity Crisis in Feminist Theory', *Signs* 13 (1988).

Alcoff, Linda, 'The Problem of Speaking for Others', *Cultural Critique* 20 (1991–2), 5–32.

Anderson, Linda, 'At the Threshold of the Self' in Moira Monteith ed. *Women's Writing: A Challenge to Theory* (Hemel Hempstead, Harvester Wheatsheaf, 1986), 54–71.

Anderson, Linda, 'The Re-Imagining of History in Contemporary Women's Fiction' in Linda Anderson ed. *Plotting Change: Contemporary Women's Fiction* (London, Edward Arnold, 1990), 129–41.

Ascher, Carol, DeSalvo, Louise and Ruddick, Sarah eds, *Between Women* (Boston, Beacon Press, 1984).

Barthes, Roland, 'Deliberation' in *A Barthes Reader* ed. Susan Sontag (London, Jonathan Cape, 1982)

Barthes, Roland, *Camera Lucida* (London, Fontana, 1984).

Barthes, Roland, 'The Death of the Author' (1968), reprinted in Philip Rice and Patricia Waugh eds *Modern Literary Theory: A Reader* (London, Edward Arnold, 1989).

Beddoe, Deirdre, *Back to Home and Duty: Women Between the Wars 1918–1939* (London, Pandora, 1989).

Bell, Alan ed. *Sir Lesle Stephen's Mausoleum Book* (Oxford, Clarendon, 1977).

Belsey, Catherine, *Critical Practice* (London, Methuen, 1980).

Beneveniste, Emile, *Problems in General Linguistics* (Florida, University of Miami Press, 1971).

Benjamin, Walter, *Illuminations* (London, Fontana, 1973).

Benstock, Shari, *The Private Self: Women's Autobiographical Writing* (London, Routledge, 1988).

Bernheimer, Charles and Kahane, Claire eds, *In Dora's Case,* (London, Virago, 1985).

Bowlby, Rachel, *Virginia Woolf: Feminist Destinations* (Oxford, Basil Blackwell, 1988).

Blunden, Edmund, *Undertones of War* (Harcourt, Brace & World, New York, 1965)

Brittain, Vera, *Testament of Youth* (London, Victor Gollancz, 1933; London, Virago, 1978)

Brittain, Vera, *Testament of Experience* (London, Victor Gollancz, 1957).

Brittain, Vera, *Chronicle of a Friendship: Vera Brittain's Diary of the Thirties 1932–1939* ed. Alan Bishop (London, Gollancz, 1986).

Brodski, Bella and Schenck, Celeste eds, *Life/Lines* (Ithaca and London, Cornell University Press, 1988).

Brooks Peter, 'Freud's Masterplot: Questions of Narrative', *Yale French Studies* 55/56 (1977), 280–300.

Broughton, Trev Lynn, 'Making the Most of Martyrdom: Harriet Matineau, Autobiography and Death', *Literature and History* 2 (1993), 24–45.

Burke, Carolyn, Schor Naomi and Whitford, Margaret, *Engaging with Irigaray* (New York, Columbia University Press, 1994).

Caruth, Cathy, 'Introduction', *American Imago* 48 (1991), 47–424

Caruth, Cathy and Deborah Esch eds, *Critical Encounters: Reference and Responsibility in Deconstructive Writing* (New Brunswick, New Jersey, Rutgers University Press, 1995).

Cixous, Hélène 'Castration or Decapitation', *Signs* 7, (1981), 41–55.

Cixous, Hélène 'Extreme Fidelity' in Susan Sellers ed. *Writing Differences: Reading from the Seminars of Hélène Cixous* (Milton Keynes, Open University Press, 1988).

Cixous, Hélène *Three Steps on the Ladder of Writing* (New York, Columbia University Press, 1993).

Cixous, Hélène and Clément, Catherine, *The Newly Born Woman*, 1975; trans Betsy Wing (Minneapolis, University of Minnesota Press, 1986).

Cobley, Evelyn, 'History and Ideology in Autobiographical Literature of the First World War', *Mosaic* 23 (1990), 37–54.

Collecott, Diana, 'Framing the *Portrait of a Lady*', *Writing Women* 1 (1981), 66–79; revised version in Singh Amritjit and Paniker Ayyapa eds *The Magic Circle of Henry James* (New York, Envoy Press, 1988).

Coward, Rosalind, *Female Desire: Women's Sexuality Today* (London, Paladin, 1984).

Dahl, Christopher, 'Virginia Woolf's *Moments of Being* and Autobiographical Tradition in the Stephen Family', *Journal of Modern Literature* 10 (1983), 175–96.

de Man, Paul 'Autobiography as Defacement', *Modern Language Notes* 94 (1979), 919–30.

de Man, Paul, *Blindness and Insight* (London, Methuen, 1993).

Du Plessis, Rachel Blau, *Writing Beyond the Ending* (Bloomington, Indiana University Press, 1985).

Edel, Leon and Gordon, N. eds, *The House of Fiction: Essays on the Novel* (London, Rupert Hart-Davis, 1957).

Edel, Leon and Ray, Gordon, N. eds, *Henry James and H.G. Wells* (London, Rupert Hart-Davis, 1958).

Ehrenreich, Barbara and English, Deirdre, *For Her Own Good* (London, Pluto Press, 1979).

Ellmann, Maud, *The Hunger Artists: Starving, Writing and Imprisonment* (Cambridge, Harvard University Press, 1993).

Feinstein, Howard, *Becoming William James* (Ithaca, Cornell University Press, 1984).

Felman, Shoshana, *What Does A Woman Want: Reading and Sexual Difference* (Baltimore and London, Johns Hopkins University Press, 1993).

Felski, Rita, *Beyond Feminist Aesthetics* (London, Hutchinson Radius, 1989).

Ferrer, Daniel, *Virginia Woolf and the Madness of Language* trans Geoffrey Bennington and Rachel Bowlby (London, Routledge, 1990).

Freud, Sigmund, 'Moses and Monotheism', The Pelican Freud Library, 13, 1974.

Freud, Sigmund, 'Mourning and Melancholia', The Pelican Freud Library, 11. 1974.

Freud, Sigmund, and Breuer, Joseph, *Studies in Hysteria* The Pelican Freud Library, 1974.

Fuss, Diana ed. *Inside/Outside: Lesbian Theories, Gay Theories* (New York, Routledge, 1991).

Fussell, Paul, *The Great War and Modern Memory* (Oxford, Oxford University Press, 1975).

Gagnier, Regenia, *Subjectivities: A History of Self-Representation in Britain, 1832–1920* (Oxford, Oxford University Press, 1991).

Gallop, Jane, *Thinking Through the Body* (New York, Columbia University Press, 1988).

Gilbert, Sandra and Gubar, Susan, *No Man's Land: The Place of the Woman Writer in the Twentieth Century*, vol 1, (New Haven and London, Yale University Press, 1988)

Gilmore, Leigh, *Autobiographics: A Feminist Theory of Women's Self-Representation* (Ithaca and London, Cornell University Press, 1994).

Gledhill, Christine ed., *Home is Where the Heart Is* (London, British Film Institute, 1987).

Gordon, Lyndall, *Virginia Woolf: A Writer's Life* (Oxford, Oxford University Press, 1984).

Grosz, Elizabeth, *Sexual Subversions: Three French Feminists* (Sydney, Allen and Unwin, 1989).

Grosz, Elizabeth, *Jaques Lacan: A Feminist Introduction* (London, Routledge, 1990).

Grosz, Elizabeth, *Space, Time, and Perversion* (London and New York, Routledge, 1995).

Gubar, Susan, '"The Blank Page" and the Issues of Female Creativity' in *Writing and Sexual Difference* ed. Elizabeth Abel (Hemel Hempstead, Harvester Wheatsheaf, 1982), 73–93.

Gusdorf, George, 'Conditions and Limits of Autobiography' in James Olney ed. *Autobiography: Essays Theoretical and Critical* (Princeton, Princeton University Press, 1980).

Harari, Josue ed., *Textual Strategies: Perspectives in Post-Structuralist Criticism* (Ithaca, Cornell University Press, 1979).

Hertz, Neil, *The End of the Line* (New York, Columbia University Press, 1985).

Higgonet, Margaret Randolph *et al.* eds, *Behind the Lines: Gender and the Two World Wars* (New Haven and London, Yale University Press, 1987), 60–7.

Hocks, Richard A., *Henry James and Pragmatic Thought* (Berkeley, University of California, 1974).

Hyman, Virginia, 'Reflections in the Looking-Glass: Leslie Stephen and Virginia Woolf', *Journal of Modern Literature* 10 (1983), 197–216.

Irigaray, Luce, 'And The One Does not Stir without The Other' *Signs* 7 (1981).

Irigaray, Luce, *This Sex Which Is Not One* (Ithaca, Cornell University Press, 1985).

Irigaray, Luce, *Speculum of the Other Woman* (Ithaca, Cornell University Press, 1985).

Irigaray, Luce, 'Volume Without Contours' in Margaret Whitford ed. *The Irigaray Reader* (Oxford, Blackwell, 1991).

Irigaray, Luce, *Sexes and Genealogies* (New York, Columbia University Press, 1993).

Jacobus, Mary, 'Beyond Determinism: George Eliot and Virginia Woolf' in *Women Writing and Writing About Women* ed Mary Jacobus (Croom Helm, London, 1979).

Jacobus, Mary, *Reading Woman: Essays in Feminist Criticism* (New York, Columbia University Press, 1986).

Jacobus, Mary, '"The Third Stroke"': Reading Woolf with Freud' in Susan Sheridan ed. *Grafts* (London, Verso, 1988), 93–110.

James, Alice, Unpublished Letters, Houghton Library, Harvard University.

James, Alice, Unpublished Letters, The National Library of Scotland.

James, Alice, ed. Edel, Leon, *The Diary of Alice James* (Harmondsworth, Penguin, 1982).

James, Henry, *The Art of the Novel* ed. Richard P. Blackmur (London, Charles Scribner, 1935).

James, Henry, *Henry James: Autobiography* (London, W.H. Allen, 1956).

James, Henry, *Letters* ed. Leon Edel, 3 vols (London, Macmillan, 1974).

James, William, *The Varieties of Religious Experience* (Harmondsworth, Penguin, 1982).

James, William, *Essays in Psychology* (Cambridge, Harvard University Press, 1983).

Jardine, Alice and Smith, Paul eds, *Men in Feminism* (New York, Methuen, 1987).

Jeffreys, Sheila, *The Spinster and Her Enemies* (London, Pandora, 1985).

Jelinek, Estelle, *The Tradition of Women's Autobiography: From Antiquity to the Present* (Boston, Twayne, 1986).

Johnson, Barbara, 'My Monster/My Self', *Diacritics* 12 (1982), 2–10.

Kamuf, Peggy, 'Penelope at Work: Interruptions in *A Room of One's Own*', Novel (1982), 5–18.

Klein, Melanie, *Love, Guilt and Reparation and Other Works 1921–1945* (London, The Hogarth Press, 1975).

Kristeva, Julia, 'Motherhood According to Giovanni Bellini' in *Desire in Language* (Oxford, Basil Blackwell, 1980).

Kristeva, Julia, 'Woman Can Never Be Defined', *Tel Quel*, 1974; extract in *New French Feminisms* ed. Elaine Marks and Isabelle de Courtivron (Hemel Hempstead, Harvester Wheatsheaf, 1981).

Kristeva, Julia, *Powers of Horror: An Essay on Abjection* trans Leon S. Roudiez (New York, Columbia University Press, 1982).

Kristeva, Julia, 'Women's Time' in *The Kristeva Reader* ed. Toril Moi (Oxford, Basil Blackwell, 1986).

Kristeva, Julia, 'About Chinese Women' in *The Kristeva Reader*.

Kristeva, Julia, 'Revolution in Poetic Language' in *The Kristeva Reader*.

Kristeva, Julia, *Black Sun: Depression and Melancholia* (New York, Columbia University Press, 1989).

Kristeva, Julia, 'A Question of Subjectivity – An Interview', *Women's Review* 12; reprinted in Phillip Rice and Patricia Waugh eds *Modern Literary Theory: A Reader* (London, Edward Arnold, 1989).

Lang, Candace, 'Autobiography in the Aftermath of Romanticism', *Diacritics* 12 (Winter, 1982), 2–16.

Lauretis, Teresa de, *Technologies of Gender* (London Macmillan, 1987).

Leaska, Michael A., *A Passionate Apprenticeship: The Early Journals 1897–1909*, (London, The Hogarth Press, 1990).

Leavis, Q.D., 'Caterpillars of the World Unite', *Scrutiny* (September, 1938), 210–11.

Lee, Hermione, 'A Burning Glass: Reflection in Virginia Woolf' in Eric Warner ed. *Virginia Woolf: A Centenary Perspective* (London, Macmillan, 1984).

Leed, Eric, *No Man's Land: Combat and Identity in World War 1* (Cambridge, Cambridge University Press, 1979).

Le Guin, Ursula, *The Dispossessed* (London, Granada, 1975).

Lejeune, Philippe, 'The Autobiographical Contract' in Tzevtan Todorov ed. *French Literary Theory Today: A Reader* (Cambridge, Cambridge University Press, 1982).

Leys, Ruth, 'Traumatic Cures: Shell Shock, and the Question of Memory', *Critical Inquiry* 20 (1994), 623–62.

Light, Alison, '"Returning to Manderley"–Romance Fiction, Female Sexuality and Class', in Mary Eagleton ed. *Feminist Literary Theory* (Oxford, Blackwell, 1986).

Lorde, Audre, *Zami: A New Spelling of My Name* (New York, Crossing Press, 1983).

Lorde, Audre, *Sister Outsider* (New York, Crossing Press, 1984).

Lorde, Audre, *A Burst of Light* (Ithaca, New York, Firebrand Books, 1988).

Marcus, Laura, 'Personal Criticism and the Autobiographical Turn' in Sally Ledger, Josephine McDonagh and Jane Spencer eds *Political Gender: Texts and Contexts* (Hemel Hempstead, Harvester Wheatsheaf, 1994).

Miller, Nancy, *The Heroine's Text: Readings in the French and English Novel, 1722–1782*, (New York, Columbia University Press, 1981).

Miller, Nancy, *Subject to Change: Reading Feminist Writing* (New York, Columbia University Press, 1988).

Miller, Nancy, *Getting Personal* (London and New York, Routledge, 1991).

Milner, Marion, *On Not Being Able To Paint* (Los Angeles, J.P. Tarcher, 1958).

Milner, Marion, *The Hands of the Living God* (London, The Hogarth Press, 1969).

Minow-Pinkney, Makiko, *Virginia Woolf and the Problem of the Subject* (Hemel Hempstead, Harvester Wheatsheaf, 1987).

Mitchell, Juliet, *Women: The Longest Revolution* (London, Virago, 1984):

Modleski, Tania, *Loving With A Vengeance: Mass-Produced Fantasies For Women* (London, Methuen, 1982).

Modleski, Tania, *Feminism Without Women: Culture and Criticism in a 'Postfeminist' Age* (London and New York, Routledge, 1991).

Nusbaum, Felicity, *The Autobiographical Subject: Gender and Ideology in Eighteenth-Century England* (Baltimore and London, Johns Hopkins University Press, 1989).

Oakley, Anne and Mitchell, Juliet eds, *The Rights and Wrongs of Woman* (Harmondsworth, Penguin, 1976).

Olney, James, *Autobiography: Essays Theoretical and Critical* (Princeton, Princeton University Press, 1980).

Ouditt, Sharon, *Fighting Forces, Writing Women* (London, Routledge, 1993).

Plath, Sylvia, *The Bell Jar* (London, Faber, 1963).

Plath, Sylvia, *Letters Home: Correspondence 1950–1963* ed. Aurelia Schober Plath (London, Faber, 1976).

Plath, Sylvia, *The Journals of Sylvia Plath* ed. Frances McCullough with Ted Hughes (New York, Ballantine Books, 1982).

Pugh, Martin, *Women and The Women's Movement in Britain 1914–1959* (London, Macmillan, 1992).

Radford, Jean ed. *The Progress of Romance: The Politics of Popular Fiction* (London, Routledge, 1986).

Radstone, Susannah, 'Remembering Medea: The Uses of Nostalgia', *Critical Quarterly* 35 (1993), 54–63.

Raitt, Suzanne, '"The Tide of Ethel": Femininity as Narrative in the Friendship of Ethel Smyth and Virginia Woolf', *Critical Quarterly* 30 (1988), 3–21.

Rich, Adrienne, *Of Lies, Secrets and Silence* (London, Virago, 1980).

Rich, Adrienne, *Of Woman Born* (London, Virago, 1977); with a new introduction, 1986.

Rich, Adrienne, *Of Blood, Bread and Poetry* (London, Virago, 1987).

Rintala, Marvin, 'Chronicler of a Generation: Vera Brittain's Testament', *Journal of Political and Military Sociology* 12 (1984), 23–35.

Roe, Sue, *Writing and Gender: Virginia Woolf's Writing Practice* (Hemel Hempstead, Harvester Wheatsheaf, 1990).

Rose, Gillian, *Feminism and Geography* (Cambridge, Polity Press, 1993).

Rose, Phyllis, *Woman of Letters* (London, Pandora, 1978).

Rose, Jacqueline, 'Jeffrey Masson and Alice James', *Oxford Literary Review* 8 (1986), 185–92.

Rose, Jacqueline, *The Haunting of Sylvia Plath* (London, Virago, 1991).

Rose, Jacqueline, *Why War?* (Oxford, Blackwell, 1994).

Ross, Andrew, *No Respect: Intellectuals and Popular Culture* (London, Routledge, 1989).

Sassoon, Seigfried, *Memoirs of an Infantry Officer* (London, Faber, 1965).

Schor, Naomi, 'Reading Double: Sand's Difference' in Nancy K. Miller ed. *The Poetics of Gender* (New York, Columbia University Press, 1986).

Schor, Naomi *Bad Objects: Essays Popular and Unpopular* (Durham and London, Duke University Press, 1995).

Scott, Joan W., 'Deconstructing Equality-Versus-Difference' in Marianne Hirsch and Evelyn Fox Keller eds *Conflicts in Feminism* (London and New York, Routledge, 1990).

Sedgewick, Eve Kokofsky, *The Epistemology of the Closet* (Hemel Hempstead, Harvester Wheatsheaf 1991).

Showalter, Elaine, *A Literature of Their Own* (London, Virago, 1978).

Smith, Sidonie, *A Poetics of Women's Autobiography* (Bloomington, Indiana University Press, 1987).

Smith, Sidonie, *Subjectivity, Identity and the Body: Women's Autobiographical Practices in the Twentieth Century* (Bloomington and Indianapolis, Indiana University Press, 1993).

Smith, Sidonie and Watson, Julia eds, *De/Colonizing the Subject: The Politics of Gender in Women's Autobiography* (Minneapolis, University of Minnesota Press, 1992).

Smith-Rosenberg, Carroll, *Disorderly Conduct* (Oxford, Oxford University Press, 1985).

Sontag, Susan ed., *A Barthes Reader* (London, Jonathan Cape, 1982).

Spivak, Gayatri Chakravorty, *Outside in the Teaching Machine* (London and New York, Routledge, 1993).

Stanley, Liz, *The Auto/Biographical I* (Manchester, Manchester University Press, 1992).

Stanton, Domna, ed., *The Female Autograph* (New York, New York Literary Forum, 1984).

Stevenson, Anne 'Writing as a Woman' in *Women Writing and Writing About Women* ed. Mary Jacobus (London, Croom Helm, 1979).

Strouse, Jean, *Alice James: A Biography*, (London, Bantam Books, 1980).

Sturrock, John, 'The New Model Autobiographer', *New Literary History* 9 (1977–8), 51–63.

Swanwick, Helena, *I Have Been Young* (London, Victor Gollancz, 1935).

Tintner, Adeline R, 'Autobiography as Fiction', *Twentieth Century Literature* 23 (1977), 239–59.

Wagner, Linda, *Sylvia Plath: The Critical Heritage*, (London and New York, Routledge, 1988).

Waters, Lindsay and Godzich, Wlad eds., *Reading de Man Reading* (Minneapolis, University of Minnesota Press, 1989).

Weed, Elizabeth, *Coming to Terms: Feminism, Theory, Politics* (London and New York, Routledge, 1989).

Whitford, Margaret, *Luce Irigaray: Philosophy in the Feminine* (London, Routledge, 1991).

Winnicott, D.W., 'Fear of Breakdown', *International Review of Psychoanalysis* 1 (1974).

Winnicott, D.W., 'Playing: The Search for the Self' in *Playing and Reality* (Harmondsworth, Penguin, 1980).

Wolf, Christa, 'The Reader and the Writer' in *The Reader and the Writer* (Berlin, Seven Seas Books, 1977).

Wolf, Christa, *The Quest for Christa T.* (London, Virago, 1982).

Woolf, Virginia, *A Room of One's Own* (London, Hogarth Press 1929; London, Granada, 1977).

Woolf, Virginia, *Collected Essays*, 4 vols (London, The Hogarth Press, 1967).

Woolf, Virginia, *Moments of Being* ed. Jeanne Schulkind (London, Granada, 1978).

Woolf, Virginia, *The Letters* ed. Nigel Nicolson, 6 vols (London, The Hogarth Press, 1980).

Woolf, Virginia, *The Diary of Virginia Woolf* ed. Anne Oliver Bell, 5 vols (London, The Hogarth Press, 1982; Harmondsworth, Penguin, 1983).

Woolf, Virginia, *A Passionate Apprenticeship; The Early Journals 1897–1909* ed. Mitchell A. Leaska (London, The Hogarth Press, 1990).

Yeazell, Ruth Bernard ed., *The Death and Letters of Alice James* (Brekeley, University of California Press, 1981).

Index